A Raft in the Pool

To MRS. I. CAMPBELL

from

John A.W. Strachan.

A Raft in the Pool

John A.W. Strachan

The Shetland Times Ltd.
Lerwick
2005

A Raft in the Pool

Copyright © John A.W. Strachan, 2005.

ISBN 1 904746 11 X

First published by The Shetland Times Ltd., 2005.

British Library Cataloguing-in-Publication Data
A catalogue record for this book is available from the British
Library.

Printed and published by
The Shetland Times Ltd.,
Gremista, Lerwick,
Shetland ZE1 0PX, UK.

To Alexandra
for her patient and unfailing support of my writing
over many years.

Contents

Illustrations

Acknowledgements

Poem – The Raft

Illustrations

Acknowledgements

My thanks are due to those people who produced photographs when I most needed them: Rose Cann, Hamish Strachan, Joyce Strachan, David Strachan, Vina Houston and Martin Leask.

The Raft

I saw a raft go floating by
On deep blue sea neath sunblessed sky
To come to rest on golden sand,
And stay a while in memories land.

This raft it floated here and there,
To ground on sand or dark seaware.
And move again when tide advanced
Like a living thing on wavelets danced.

Our lives are like that restless raft
Sailing on like mindless craft.
Fetching up on unknown shore
Then wandering on again once more.

So as you sail along life's way
Recall with me the seablown spray,
The hazy days of summers gone
When water splashed and bright sun shone.

And you the raft in life's blue sea,
Yondering on forever free.
Never resting, seldom tired
With a zest for life inspired.

John A. W. Strachan

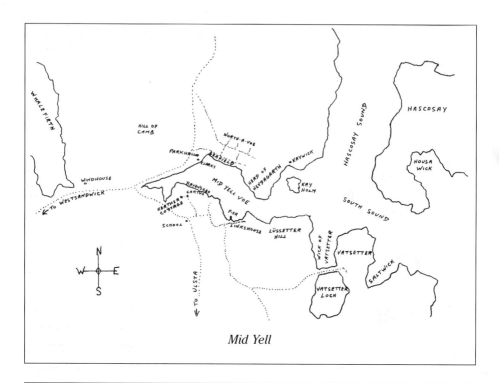

Mid Yell

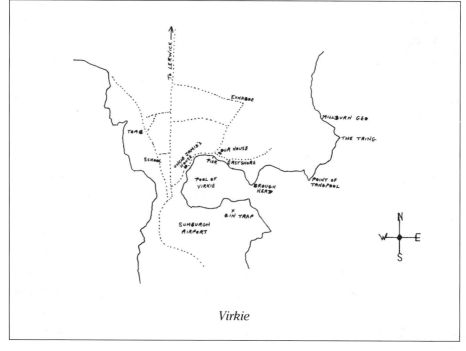

Virkie

Chapter One

Heather Cottage Days

One of my earliest escapades came when I was some months short of my second birthday. It is a good age for getting into a variety of unusual places, especially when unobserved by busy adults.

On this occasion I managed to get under, or behind, our old organ where my father, home on leave from the merchant navy, had secreted a half-bottle of black rum as a reserve supply for the New Year festivities.

Somehow I pulled the cork out of the bottle and began to enjoy myself. I don't know how much I consumed, but when I was discovered there were grown-up fears as to what such potent spirits would do to my tender insides. Me? I was not in the least bothered. By then I was probably lost in a happy, if drunken, little world of my own. Whatever, I had the best and longest sleep any baby ever enjoyed and I can't recall suffering any hangover symptoms.

After that liquid encounter I was not to taste alcohol again until I was in my early twenties, and, when I did sample the 'demon drink' again, I found I preferred the taste of black rum ... had I been influenced by that early encounter?

This was wartime and one of the sounds that became familiar to us was the drone of aircraft engines. Ours we liked and would wave wildly to the pilots ... theirs we hated and feared. But that did not stop us from running outside at the first distant sound, a fact that must have had our mother in a state of constant worry.

One day when we heard an approaching plane she was working on a circular knitting machine making socks for the war effort. She attempted to forestall our rush for the door by claiming the sound was coming from her machine. Hamish was more than two years older than I, and, even had I been fooled, he certainly was not.

"It's a plane!" he shouted, heading for the door at speed.

The author's father, Thomas (Tammie) Johnston Strachan.

We arrived outside just in time to wave to the pilot of a Catalina flying boat as it thundered overhead not a great many feet above the roof.

Heather Cottage was a little stone-built house up on the hillside overlooking the head of Mid Yell Voe. The voe was a good sheltered anchorage for a variety of vessels, which would surely have been a draw for any stray enemy aircraft.

One day we heard a sound like someone running a stick along corrugated iron. Uncle Harold, one of Dad's six brothers, often made that sound when he was home on leave and came to visit us, and thinking he was home again we ran to meet him. Mum knew better and tried to stop us, but evading her desperately reaching arms, and ignoring her shouted warnings, we raced for the great outdoors to greet our uncle.

There was no one at the door and the rat-tat-tat sound came from German machine-guns. A plane had come over and attacked

Helen and Georgina Strachan; our grandmother & mother.

*Our parents' wedding, 18th March, 1937. Best man: Willie Johnson.
Bridesmaid: Bertha Leask.*

houses in Basta, a few miles north of us. Then, sweeping in over the hill, it attacked vessels lying in Mid Yell Voe. That done it sped shoreward, guns blazing, and proceeded to follow the road firing at anything in its path. The shop at Ravensgeo was hit but the plane had not turned its guns on our maternal grandparents' home.

Dad told of a narrow escape he had with an enemy aircraft while crossing Lüssetter Hill to visit his parents in Vatsetter (pronounced Vatster). He saw the plane almost as soon as he heard the distant throb of its engine, and one glance was enough to tell him it was a German and that it was heading straight for him.

German pilots had the reputation, whether earned or not, of shooting at anything that moved, and there was nowhere to hide on that bare hillside. He could do nothing but stand and watch as it hurtled towards him and be ready to duck at top speed if they opened up on him. He was sure that his last day had come. However, instead of shooting, the pilot gave him a cheerful wave.

These two stories surely show the difference between men at

war: the first was out for bullets and glory, while the second had a goodly amount of caring humanity in his heart.

We had a radio on which we heard a variety of programmes, but what I recall most clearly is Dad's fury over the broadcasts from Germany by the traitor William Joyce, who was known as 'Lord Haw-Haw'. Like so many people at the time Dad would have liked nothing better than to have got his hands on him.

The world seemed full of uniforms so it was not long before two little boys acquired soldier's hats and began to train themselves to be the bravest of the brave.

When our sister, Rose, was old enough to toddle around with us she was conscripted into our tiny army and on route marches about the fields we trained her without mercy, until one day she burst into tears, deserted her post and ran home to mother crying and claiming that, "The bowels have hitten me!" At the time she was so little that she had not quite mastered the word 'boys'.

Then one day figures were seen on the Hill of Camb, across the head of the voe. Word swiftly spread that the Germans had landed and soon a little knot of worried people gathered in front of Heather Cottage, which was the best vantage point.

We could see figures, carrying weapons of some kind, advancing over the ridge and down toward the road and seashore. Was it really Hitler and his Nazi army come to shoot us all?

"My goodness, Georgina," said Annie o' Houl to our mother, "if yon's da Nazi army dir no' very mony o' dem. I'm seen mair dan yon at a makkin." This caused a ripple of strained laughter.

There was now a great deal of chatter amongst our group as to whether this small company was an advance patrol, and if so, was the whole German army now on the other side of Camb Hill?

Someone was urging us children to go inside out of sight when the truth was brought to us: Dad's Army, the Home Guard was out on manoeuvres.

Dad was often away for long months sailing and he had several adventures himself, but there were times when his hours off watch were spent in making toys for us. Once it was a fleet of wooden warships. A destroyer had a gun that fired a cork at a larger vessel made of blocks. If the cork hit the right block the ship exploded. This explosion was achieved by means of a mousetrap built into the battleship. We spent many enjoyable hours playing with that fleet but, sadly, I doubt if it survived the war by many years and is now but a memory.

Once a ship Dad was on came to lie in Lerwick harbour and we went down to be with him while he was there. That was a great adventure, and my first visit to Lerwick, though all I can remember about it is seeing the ships in the harbour and the sound of traffic along the North Road out of town, which kept us awake at nights.

I went to school when I was four, but have no memory of that first day, or of many others during those early years. The fact that I hated school from the first day might mean that my mind has blotted it out, or has grown too lazy to recall it all again.

I do, however, remember those terrible gas masks. I doubt if any child of that time ever liked them, but with the threat of enemy planes dropping gas in our playground, parents and teachers were adamant that we learned how to wear them. Hamish flatly refused to have his on and I doubt if he ever wore one.

Hamish always enjoyed a good laugh, but I doubt if he was trying to be funny one day when a teacher was teaching his class their letters and sternly addressed him, whilst tapping each chalky letter on the blackboard with a pointer, "U-P ... up, Hamish."

"No sir," he retorted indignantly, "I pee down," and the class dissolved into giggles.

We could go to school by either of two routes: along the hill dyke and fence which was quicker but might lead to wet feet, or along the road through Gardie where we would meet up with some of our pals.

I was very shy with other children but was even worse with grown-ups. It is no wonder that I was often the one lagging behind, ever wanting to make friends but too shy to do anything about it.

I was interested in nature and often was to be found with my nose down in a puddle or ditch. Birds fascinated me and whenever I was outside would watch any I could see, even if I didn't know their names.

Pals . . . Hamish Strachan and Jim Gray, c.1940.

One day on the way to school I earned myself a nickname (thankfully of short duration) when I suddenly shouted excitedly, "A Jenny Wren! I saw a Jenny Wren!" This name I'd picked up from one of our little books. Thankfully, only a few of my pals teased me with the name, for which I was glad, for being called 'Jenny Wren' would have been much worse than being called by my initials ... JAWS.

Then came a day filled with shame and trauma when I suffered an attack of diarrhoea. As chance would have it this came upon me at playtime and when I was discovered, Hamish and his pal, Jim, went to ask the headmaster if they could take me home.

The question asked, they stood there in some awe waiting for the head to give his permission.

"Why?" asked the head.

"Because he's made a mess, sir," Hamish replied.

"A mess! What kind of a mess, boy?"

"A dirty mess, sir."

At this moment Jim was bending close to Hamish's ear telling him exactly what he should be saying, but Hamish didn't wish to earn

Proud parents take Hamish for a walk, c.1940.

the headmaster's wrath by using what he considered to be bad words.

"What kind of a dirty mess, Hamish?"

"Tell him, tell him," Jim whispered eagerly.

"A dirty stinking mess, sir," Hamish said.

At last the headmaster realised what was meant and I was taken home ... it had not been a good day for me.

Uncle John Leask, our mother's brother, was a rifleman in the 2nd Battalion Cameronians, Scottish Rifles, and was seriously wounded during the Anzio Beach campaign in 1944. He took a long time to recover well enough to come home.

We children could sense the worry and fear in our elders, not for themselves, but for loved ones far away and in danger. Then, at long last, came VE Day in 1945 and the surrender at Rheims, which ended the war in Europe.

At last people could begin to pick up their lives again and there was a degree of cheerfulness over the land, even though so many young folk would never return and others be so affected by what they had been through that they would never be quite the same again.

Everyone was looking forward to a future where there would be no more wars, no more enemy aircraft over the islands, no more bombs, mines or bullets ... only a peace that would last forever.

Chapter Two

A Place to Remember

One day, when Rose was two or three years old, we were playing some game or other outdoors, possibly marching our imaginary army about the rigs, when Mum came out to the door and, seeing only two of us, asked, "Where's Rose?"

This was a question we could not answer, for while she had been with us earlier, she had deserted her post some time before and we presumed her to have returned to the house to 'help' her mother.

We shook our heads and said we didn't know, whereupon our mother turned back to the house saying, "Oh, she'll be wi' her father." She called to Dad, who was home on leave, "Tammie, is Rose there?"

"No. She's no' here," Dad replied from further inside the house. "Is she no' wi' the boys?"

"No," Mum said, a note of worry in her voice. "Where is she?"

A quick check inside showed that she wasn't to be seen in any of the rooms so they came outside and we all began to call her name ... no answer.

Heather Cottage was a good way up the hill from the sea, but worries began to be expressed that she might have wandered down the hill towards the beach. However, a search of the beach showed no sign of her. By now Hamish had been sent to fetch Daa, our maternal grandfather Andrew Leask, who was a reserve policeman at the time. After making sure Rose hadn't been found he called out the Home Guard and the search widened.

Our mother by this time was so distraught that she returned weeping to the house, convinced that harm had come to her little girl and she was lost forever.

In the living room she suddenly heard a sound ... what could it be? Then, hardly daring to breath, she approached Dad's sea chest.

Uncle Harold ploughs a furrow.

The faint sound had come from there. With hope suddenly bounding in her heart she reached down and raised the lid.

Lying there, her cheeks flushed with sleep, was the object of the search. What relief was felt by the searchers when the call came: "She's here. She's found. Asleep in her Dad's sea chest."

Once, Dad arrived home with a monkey whom we called Jeanie. We loved that cheeky little 'person' although some of the neighbourhood ladies were very wary of her. Especially after she escaped one bright summer day, climbed to the highest point, and pelted two of them with anything she could find as they were passing on their way to work in the peat hill. Needless to say the ladies kilted up their skirts and took to their heels in terror.

If Jeanie had a failing it was an eagerness to eat anything small that came her way. Her careless eating habits meant that whenever she was allowed the run of the house any tiny items had to be hidden.

Although we were all very careful to keep such things as buttons, Saccharines etc., out of her sight, I fear that her love of indigestible food led to an early death.

We wept bitterly when she died after eating a tiny bottle of dye, but perhaps her time with us taught us all the folly of trying to keep any animal without knowing all about them and their dietary requirements.

If Jeanie had loved any of us then it might have been Rose, and if Hamish or myself pretended to bully her, Jeanie would become angry and hang on the wire of her cage chattering at us.

Heather Cottage had its share of wild life including 'slaters' (woodlice) and 'forkietails' (earwigs). We were very wary of forkietails after being told how Uncle Bertie Strachan had got one in his ear when a boy, and suffered much pain and discomfort until the doctor spat some tobacco juice into the ear to kill it. The forkietail was removed the following day ... we certainly did not want them near our ears.

There were also 'hundiclocks' (large black beetles), but most

Uncle Harold and Bobby take a nap.

numerous were the big black hill spiders that would climb over the walls and ceiling ready to lower themselves floorwards at any minute. They were harmless, but two naughty little boys terrified their sister by telling her that the spiders would lower themselves down on her when she was asleep. No wonder Rose has never liked spiders.

There were also hill mice, but not in large numbers, thanks, perhaps, to our feline friend Diamond, so called because of a diamond of white on his black head.

One Sunday Mum was cooking a roast for dinner. These were hard times and a roast, even a small one, was a splendid treat for us. The lovely aroma of roasting flesh had us boys, playing just outside the door, licking our lips in anticipation. None of us realised that another, crinkling his feline nose, was also intent on that scent.

Slowly, Diamond moved to the door and crept inside. Waiting until the cook's attention was taken with something else, he pounced onto the table where the roast had just been set and began to eat.

Suddenly Mum screamed to Dad that the cat was at the roast. Diamond shot out the door, heading at top speed for a hole some distance from the house, which he shied off to in times of trouble.

Dad picked up the first thing that came to hand – a tin of distemper he'd bought to paint the walls with – and, enraged by the theft, hurled it after the speeding miscreant. The tin hit the ground and burst open an instant before Diamond disappeared down his bolthole.

It had not been Dad's best day. Not only had his dinner been stolen, but he'd lost the contents of his tin too. However, it pleased him to think that some of it was now possibly on the thief ... just going to show that, even when it costs you dear, revenge can be sweet.

It was some time before Diamond came near the house again, especially when Dad was there.

On days when we could not venture out because of the weather we spent a lot of time gazing out the window. From our vantage point we could see any vehicles on the north side of the voe. Very infrequent they were too, there being few motor cars in Yell at that time.

When nothing was to be seen outside but a curtain of lashing rain, sleet or hail, we often played at racing raindrops down the panes.

Hamish had a fine singing voice and, just after the war, he began singing in public and became very popular. Thankfully, my voice was nothing to brag about so I was spared from having to face a hall full of people. There was one time, however, when I was persuaded to sing or recite 'Jesus Loves Me' for a Sunday School concert.

It just so happened that shortly before this event we became the proud owners of a set of chest expanders. During my moment of stardom, when I came to the words "I am weak, but He is strong", I put a great deal of emphasis on the last word, and stretching out my arms gave a fine demonstration of the strong man whose picture adorned the box of our chest expanders set.

Daa (grandfather) was a frequent visitor and we always enjoyed his company. One of my earliest recollections is of him carrying baby Rose around singing 'Sleep Kentucky Babe'. Very likely we boys received the same treatment when we were babies for he was a very kind-hearted man.

When Uncle Harold went away to sea he sometimes left his pony with us. We loved having Bobby at Heather Cottage and I have fond memories of us bringing home the peats with pony power.

Sometimes we would hear the sound of someone entering the porch, and on investigating would find the visitor to have a large nose, four legs and a tail. The clever animal had soon learned that the porch door opened with a latch, and knew that if he lifted the latch and walked into the porch he might get a scolding from Mum, but would very likely be tempted outside again with some titbit or other.

Being Uncle Harold's pony, Bobby was so well trained that he could have put any circus horse to shame. He could bow, shake hands, play dead and count up to ten. In fact, it seemed that with Harold as trainer, Bobby could do almost everything but talk.

One day our paternal grandfather, also John Strachan, who lived a few miles away in Vatsetter, decided to take his boat up onto the beach to make repairs and do a paint job on her, but she was too large for men to pull up and he realised that it was a job for Bobby.

Tammie Strachan, the Wreck and the Vatsetter dog,
Frank

The problem was that Harold was several thousand miles away on a ship bound for somewhere exotic. Grandfather felt that he was getting too old for chasing ponies about the hills of East Yell so Uncle Bertie, who had been discharged from the merchant navy in 1944 due to chest trouble, was called on to go and fetch the pony from the hill ... but where in the hills would the pony be?

Someone recalled seeing ponies away over towards Aywick, which lies south of Vatsetter, so Bertie set off. About an hour later he came on a herd of ponies up behind the hill dykes of Aywick, but which pony was Bobby?

With so many animals there were several that might have been Bobby, but Bertie just could not decide which was the one he wanted. Whistling didn't bring the desired result, nor did any of the commands he tried ... Bobby probably realised there was work afoot and was hiding amongst all his friends.

What was Uncle Bertie to do?

Suddenly an idea stirred in his mind. Going as close to the herd as he could he asked quietly, "Would any o' you folk lik' a slice o' bread?"

Only one pony responded and he knew right away that the one standing nodding his head was the one he sought. Uncle Harold had always asked that question and the well-trained Bobby knew well enough that nodding would get him his food ... this time, however, it also got him some jolly hard work.

Yet Bobby was not destined to spend his remaining years roaming the hills of East Yell. Harold eventually took him south to fine green fields in east Scotland and for some years thereafter, when he came home from sea, he would pause on his way north to visit Bobby, who would greet him gladly then go through the many tricks he'd learned on the Links of Vatsetter, happy to be with his friend and master again.

Soon after the war Dad gave up the sea and settled down to work on a road gang in Yell. Model yacht racing was popular and he was a splendid hand at making Shetland models. Once he made one out of wreck-wood a neighbour had found and given to Daa, who gave it to Dad. It became a fine little craft called *The Wreck* and she was destined to win several races.

We were always delighted to accompany our elders to the races, which were enjoyable outings for the whole family. They were held at various lochs in Yell. It was fine to see a fleet of beautifully built yachts speeding along before the wind and it always surprised me how excited grown-ups could become as their yachts neared the winning point.

Over the years Dad was to make several very fine vessels, but *The Wreck*, *Mayflower*, *Rosina* and *Victory* were the ones I knew best.

One day, three little rascals took a small yacht, possibly the

Victory, down to the beach with the intention of sailing it in the shallows along the shore. However, Dad's yachts always had good deep keels so we required a depth of water to sail it in which meant letting it go further offshore to deeper water.

All might have gone smoothly had we attached a string to her, but we had overlooked this fact so when she suddenly took a starboard tack and headed for the distant (to us little ones) shores of North-a-Voe there seemed no way we could alter her course.

Had we been older we could have run around the head of the voe and fetched her back, but being much too small and inexperienced for that we resorted to stones. We only realised the rashness of that method of trying to alter her course when our brave little ship began to sink ... perhaps one of the stones had done more than splash down beside the yacht. Sadly, we stood there watching as she disappeared below the surface.

Dad was quite cross about that, and we were forbidden to use any of his yachts in such a way again. Later, the wreck of the yacht was found washed up on the far shore and repaired.

I cannot speak for the others, but I was sorry to leave the place of my birth. Mind you, I can understand the necessity, as Heather Cottage was very small for raising a family in.

These days I often feel a little 'hot under the collar' when I see so many empty and ruinous houses about the islands, but when I visit the ruins of Heather Cottage I think of what fine memories lie hidden in the rubble of its walls ... and I'm off remembering again.

Chapter 3

Camb and Reafirth

It seemed strange to be living almost straight across the voe from Heather Cottage in a building that had once been Clark's shop, some yards in front of a larger house called Park Hall.

Here, we just had to step out the door and walk around the corner and we were almost on the beach. We spent much of our free time splashing about in the sea.

Often Dad and some of our neighbours would row across the voe to the shop at Ravensgeo for the weekend shopping. We sometimes went with them but I was not there the day Dad lost his pipe, and I learned the following story from our friend John Williamson.

The old pier at Ravensgeo was beginning to fall apart, but the most dangerous part may have been the slipway at which we would land. It lived up to the first part of the name by being covered, at sea level, with slime and seaweed, a place where one had to tread very carefully.

On this day, after visiting the shop, they returned to the boat and clambered aboard again. One of the men called to a young lad on the slip asking him to loosen the mooring rope and throw it aboard.

Dad had just lit his pipe and was taking the first few draws on it when the wildly thrown mooring rope whipped it out of his mouth and over the side where, with a plop and a sizzle, it was effectively extinguished.

Dad's comments on this occasion are best left unrecorded but they left the young fellow on the slipway in no doubt of what was thought of his marksmanship. However, Dad was never one to hold onto his anger when he could let it go in laughter so he quickly saw the funny side of it and was soon laughing with the rest.

There were times, too, when we would go to visit our relations

Linkshouse, Mid Yell.

in Vatsetter, about two miles on the east side of Mid Yell. It had been a shorter walk when we lived on the other side of the voe as we could walk down through Gardie and on to Linkshouse, from where the path led up by Lüssetter Manse, on over the Hill of Lüssetter and down into one of the most attractive areas in Yell.

After calling along Uncle Willie and his family in Westerhouse we would cross over the 'Links', the grassy strip of land between the loch and the sea, then up the 'King's Gaet' (path) to the houses east of the loch where we would visit each in turn.

Our grandparents' house was always a popular place and I remember Grandfather John as being a cheery old man with a white beard and a strong Doric accent, he having been born in 1868 in the east coast Scottish town of Buckanhaven. He had settled in Vatsetter after coming north to the herring fishing around 1890, but he had also been a merchant seaman. He would sing songs from the east coast and play the concertina. Sometimes, too, he would sit outside on fine summer days to play and sing his favourite hymns.

Granny, too, was a strong character with dark hair and eyes. She had not had an easy life, having lost her father, James Johnson, when she was about twelve. His ship, the barque *Anglesea*, had been

Mid Yell Voe from above Lüssetter House on the way to Vatsetter.

lost with all hands after running into a violent blizzard whilst on a voyage home from America in 1880.

Granny Helen had raised seven sons and a daughter, and having nine people to care for there must have been times when her day seemed to be all toil, but she saw that there was always food on the table when required, a warm fire glowing in the hearth and a cheery welcoming smile.

Like many women of her day with access to large amounts of water she often used to do her washing outside on fine summer days, taking it down to the loch to do the job properly. By this I don't mean that the clothes were washed in the cold, peaty loch, but she would build a fire and heat a large pot of water, then do her wash.

There is a tiny island in Vatsetter loch and we knew well the story of how some of the Strachan brothers had taken clumps of magellan ragwort, known locally as either Australian or New Zealand daisies, and planted them on the island, where they still grow today.

Of course, on a visit to Vatsetter we would have time to play with our cousins in the fields outside whilst our parents enjoyed a good yarn with the old folk and whoever else was there.

Gilbert and James Johnson, Vatsetter. James was our great grandfather. Lost with his ship 1880.

The beaches down at the Links were sand covered on both sea and loch shore and the burn running between the two was crossed by a small brig. In the spring and summer the sward would gleam with Mayflowers (primula), but sadly, due to the indiscriminate grazing of animals in recent years, the Mayflowers have gone ... another example of how sheep have destroyed much of Shetland's wild flowers.

I had a very dear friend at that time and one that went everywhere with me ... nothing more than a little felt penguin but he was as dear to me as a living friend could be and I even took him to school with me.

In these enlightened days I would probably have been allowed to keep 'Penny' until I lost interest in him, but back in the forties things were different and no one realised how much security I got from him. There were those who believed it was unhealthy for a boy of six to be carrying soft toys around and at last my elders gave in to the pressure, and one terrible day Penny disappeared.

I was inconsolable and grieved deeply for my friend. That this was a seriously traumatic event in my young life is proven by the fact that I have never forgotten Penny.

Then came the storms of 1947, with deep snow and chilling winds, when the whole country was held in the grip of an extremely

The family of John and Helen Strachan. Back: Willie, Nellie, John.
Front: Harold, Davie, Jamie, Bertie and Tammie.

hard winter. But the worst winter for half a century saw us little ones enjoying ourselves.

One day, as we returned from school, we paused to play in the partially frozen Burn of Camb. There were sheets of ice on the calmer water and some of the older boys, including Hamish, decided to test their skating and ice walking abilities, but they had not been on the ice for long when there was a crack and a couple of boys went through. It was not deep, but they got a good wetting before they were helped back to the bank.

It had been good fun, but two were not laughing, and as we walked along the banks' path to the house Hamish was leaving a trail of splashes behind him. Very likely we were both worried about the 'talking to' we'd get when Mum saw his wet clothes and realised we'd been playing in the burn.

Another day, when the snow had gone and a north-easterly gale was blowing, I found myself in serious trouble when a strong gust picked me up and plunged me headfirst into a deep ditch beside the house.

Luckily, the ditch was not full of water, for each time I attempted to climb out the wind blew me back in again. I was choking as the violence of the gale seemed to whip my breath away ... and there was my dear, big brother standing in the middle of the path, schoolbag in hand, laughing at the way the wind played with me. At last though, he realised that I really was in trouble and, grabbing my hand, pulled me out.

A great many birds died that year due to the severity of the weather and no one was more aware of this than we who lived so close to the shore. The victims lay along the beach by the dozen, in various states of decay. The condition of the carcasses, however, did not stop two little boys with sorrowing hearts from gathering all the bodies into a pile on the grassy brow of the banks not far from the house ... and in full view from the windows of Park Hall.

Time has erased our reason for collecting the dead birds, perhaps we were just tidying up, or making a count of the fallen, but whatever, our heap was growing ever larger and probably the scent of decay was spreading too, though, to be sure, it did not bother us.

Suddenly, out from Park Hall swept Mrs Spence, the lady of the house, to bear down on us with angry mien and order us, in no uncertain terms, to "Put that stinking mess back where it came from and stop fouling the air with the stench of death. Do it now or I shall lodge a serious complaint with your father."

Slowly, as we watched her erect and darkly dressed figure recede, we began to move our heap down to the beach again where the bodies lay until there was nothing left but bones. They, too, slowly disappeared into the sand to become part of the beach the birds once flew over.

Sometimes we would be taken to see a film in the hall, which was a good distance from the house. I only recall one of the films we went to see. Just after Robinson Crusoe found Man Friday's footprint in the sand there was a breakdown which could not be repaired that evening, and, as far as I know, I never did see the last part, but we knew and loved the story, having read and had it read to us many times.

Once I recall us being taken to a wedding in the south of the island. To get there we went by hired car. At one point a motorcycle whizzed by us going in the same direction. Presently the road dipped down into a valley (possibly Otterswick) before climbing up the other side. As we arrived at the top of the first hill we saw the motorcyclist racing up the next. What he could not see was a car, heading north, approaching the same corner.

There were exclamations from the grown-ups who could see what might happen as the man on the motorcycle was not wasting time. Their fears were realised when the two vehicles met and the motorcyclist went flying off the road and over the handlebars.

Our vehicle, driven by Tom Brown, crept down the road and, what seemed ages later, arrived at the scene of the accident. In a few words we learned that the people from the car were attending to the injured man and would take him to the doctor in Mid Yell. He had 'sort of' landed on his head, but was conscious and appeared to be all right.

We continued on our way and were somewhat surprised when the motorcyclist, his head swathed in bandages, was later to be

Helen Strachan with youngest son Tammie, c.1915.

Helen Strachan washing clothes at Vatsetter Loch.

seen enjoying himself at the function. Perhaps proving the old saying that you can't keep a good man down.

We now had a different cat. Diamond, like many another, refused to leave the area of his home. Maisie was a tortoiseshell, and a much better cat for children, allowing us to lift her up and carry her around. Of course, there was one drawback ... being female she was bound to have kittens which is how we presently came to have a tomcat called Daisy. He was given that feminine name for the simple reason that when he was a tiny kitten we children were sure he was a sweet-faced female.

It was while staying here that I had my only experience of taking home peats by horse and cart. On a fine summer's day the horse and cart arrived from Basta. We had much enjoyment as the cart was loaded, taken back along the road to our house, emptied, and returned for more until there were no more peats left at the bank.

We often fished from the little pier below the house. Usually we removed limpets from the rocks and out of their shells, tied a string around their middle and lowered them to the bottom. To make sure they would sink right down a small stone was tied on as a weight. Then we would watch and wait until the crabs got the scent and came to investigate. We caught lots of crabs this way.

We were often joined at this and other 'sports' by some of our pals, like John Williamson who lived further north in Colvister but sometimes spent part of his holidays near us in Camb.

Presently, however, we were on the move again. This time we returned to the south side of the voe to live in a little house in Reafirth. This building was already occupied by an old lady, Anderina Inkster, who dwelt in one end, whilst we five were crammed into the other.

She was a nice old lady who seemed to enjoy having young children around and we liked staying there even though there was hardly room for us all. My memory seems to tell me that there was a small apple tree just outside the door which actually produced small fruits, but I can't recall whether they were edible or not.

Our feline friend Maisie had not liked the move and several times we found her near the school and figured she was determined to return to her old home. One day we saw her at the top of a telegraph pole near the house and begged Dad to go and borrow a ladder from our neighbour, Tom Brown, and rescue her. Dad looked up at the cat on the pole before saying, "We'll just leave her there. Don't worry, she'll come down when she's good an' ready."

He was right too, for a short while later Maisie almost ran down the pole for a yard or two before launching herself in a magnificent leap for the ground. Landing, she did a little 'heels-up' jump and ran for the house.

A few days later we received word that Maisie had returned to her old home and moved in with Mrs Spence of Park Hall. We were very disappointed but it was useless to try to take her back.

I often wondered if she had good reason to climb the pole that day. From its top she could get the lie of the land, and from up there she would have been able to see her old home and judge exactly how to get there.

That left us with Daisy who seemed content to stay with us. Perhaps his mother considered him too young to make the journey, or else figured that if he wouldn't leave the nest ... she would.

Thinking about that time brings the scent of Plasticine to mind for we were often modelling things out of it. If ever we were given a few pennies the first thing we would do would be to run down the road to Brown's shop to buy some.

It was either modelling, painting or drawing for us when the weather kept us inside, though I was beginning to enjoy reading too, but I was mighty poor at that just yet.

I loved going into shops, even if I was so terribly shy, because the moment you entered you were almost over-powered by a variety of pungent scents. Perhaps the strongest was salt fish and carbolic soap, but it was a lovely experience to open the door and take a deep breath as you tried to identify all the different odours. How sad that today shops have lost their odorous appeal and would probably be condemned if they found it again.

Chapter Four

In the Deep South

One day we three were playing about inside the fence by the road when I, either by accident or design, pushed my little sister so that she fell against the fence. This gave her more of a fright than a hurt, but tears did flow and she disappeared in the direction of the house leaving us in no doubt that she intended to tell Mum how badly we were treating her. We followed her and in the house she went straight to Mum and cried, "Mummy, Mummy. Hamish pushed me against the fence."

Perhaps she really thought he had done it, but hearing her words he was aghast at what he thought was a bare-faced lie and shouted, "I did not. It was John Arnold. He pushed her on the fence."

"It was Hamish," Rose wailed back, pointing a finger at him, "he did it."

"It wasn't me ... "

"Stop trying to put the blame on your peerie bridder," Mum, obviously believing Rose, said to Hamish, "an' go out of here an' leave Rose alone. You're nothing better than a couple of big bullies."

"But Mum," I said, "it was me ... "

"I'll not tell you again," she interrupted sternly. "Any more lip from you two and I'll mak' sure your Dad hears about it. Now away out an' play ... at once."

"Aw come on," Hamish said to me as he cast a last scowling glance at Rose, "she's just a lyin' peerie Yickle o' the Toekle."

I don't know where we got this saying from. It may have come from the days before Rose could speak properly and complained that she had a tickle in her toe which came out as a yickle of the toekle, or it could have come from our comics, the radio, or more likely out of my big brother's fertile imagination. Whatever, it was the one thing

At North Haa, Westsandwick: Hamish, Ian Mcleod, Rose, Karl Mcleod and John A.W. Strachan in the late 1940s.

that was sure to upset Rose and have her in tears. She hated that above all things.

As we went outside again, Rose was shouting that she was not a Yickle of the Toekle and Mum was telling her to pay no attention to us. We were bad boys who would be in serious trouble when their father came home. Little did she know how true those words would prove to be.

Hamish was still smarting over being blamed for something he had not done and was determined to get his revenge.

"Just wait," he said, "'til she comes outside, we'll grab her an' teach her a lesson."

"I dunno," I muttered, "we'll get inta more trouble if we hurt her."

"We'll no' hurt her," says he, "we'll just grab her an' put a spider down her neck. That'll teach her ta tell lies."

"She's awful frightened for spiders," I said doubtfully. "It'll maybe tak' a while ta find one too."

"John Arnold," he said slowly, as if talking to someone with slow mental faculties, "we don't have ta have a real spider, we can just pretend. That'll teach her a lesson. See, I'll grab her an' you pretend ta put a spider down her neck."

I decided that maybe he was right ... after all, as far as we knew she had deliberately told a lie. So we waited and were at last rewarded by the sight of our little sister coming out the door. We waited until she was far enough out that she couldn't duck back inside again then Hamish made a dive and caught her. She squealed and fought to get away but he held her tight.

"Now, you peerie liar," he growled, "I'll teach you ta tell lies about me."

"Let me go!" she wailed, struggling gamely. "Let me go!"

"You know what we're goin' ta do?" he asked, "we're goin' ta put a hundred spiders down your lyin' peerie neck."

"No, no!" Her voice was now almost a scream.

"John Arnold, do it now," Hamish cried as he fought to hold the struggling girl.

Swiftly, I reached over and touched her neck with my fingers, as I trickled a bit of grit inside her collar. She really screamed then and upon being released ran in panic for the house. She was now in such a state of terror that even when she reached her mother she just stood there screaming.

We had followed her into the house and were now somewhat alarmed at how well our 'lesson' had worked. Our mother was demanding to know what had happened, but before we could tell her she had to bring Rose out of her blind panic which she achieved by giving her a sharp slap on the face. With Rose's frightened weeping in the background we told Mum what had happened, and by then we knew we were really in trouble.

It took Mum some time to calm Rose down and ease her fears about spiders. Rose was not at ease, however, until she had had an entire change of clothes, just to make sure I really hadn't put a spider down her neck.

So that day Hamish and I were not the most popular boys around, but there was a self-satisfied look on his face at times that told me that, despite the trouble we were in, he was pleased he'd got his revenge and taught Rose a lesson she really would never forget.

However, the term 'Yickle of the Toekle' was still used to tease Rose with until we moved away from Yell itself. Of course, we were not always bad to our little sister, and we often played happily together.

We were not to stay in Reafirth for long and were soon on the move again. Rose had become very friendly with Old Anderina and was deeply disappointed to be leaving, but in future she was to visit her friend each time she was in Mid Yell.

Our next place of residence was to be North Haa, Westsandwick, on the west coast of Yell. Here we had to attend a new school and make new friends. North Haa had a large walled garden in which we were allowed to play if we behaved ourselves. It was in that garden that I first encountered the scent of roses and even today when I come in contact with scented roses I am reminded of that garden.

There were times, too, when I would lie on the grass in the sun and watch the creatures about me. Bumble bees would buzz about on their journey from flower to flower and the fluttery flight of butterflies would at times become much more rapid as they desperately dodged the sharp beaks of hungry birds. They were usually successful and I only remember one bird catching a cabbage white.

We had to fetch our milk and eggs from a nearby farm and normally would have enjoyed the walk through the fields, but there were the geese to be avoided and to my mind these were birds to keep away from. There would be a good chance of spilt milk and broken eggs if they took after you as they often did ... these were their

Mid Yell School photo, late 1940s.
Back: Mr. Irvine, Christopher Irvine, Graham Clark, Betty Williamson, Ethel Smith, Sylvia Smith, Eleanor Irvine, George Irvine, John Clark, Miss Houston.
3rd row: Charlie Clark, Billy Smith, John A.W. Strachan, Jessamine Clark, Mabel Williamson, Jean Smith, Rosemary Brown, Jim Gray, Wilbert Johnson.
2nd row: Hamish Strachan, Gilbertha Williamson, Mary Jane Pole, Rose Strachan, Margaret Inkster, Caroline Williamson, Billy Guthrie.
1st row: John Tulloch, Charlie Inkster, Daniel Smith, Billy Williamson, Basil Guthrie, Harry Tulloch.

The house at East Shore Virkie, c.1950.

fields and no mere human offspring was going to trespass through them.

Daisy, our misnamed tomcat, was growing larger and we soon discovered that he preferred to live away up the hill feeding on whatever he could catch, rather than on what we provided. Of course we tried to persuade him to give up his wild existence and return to the fold, but as time went by he became so wild and ferocious that we were warned not even to try to catch him.

Then one day Dad found him caught in a rabbit trap. Dad, who never liked such implements of torture fetched him home, wrapped in his jacket, to tend his wounds. He managed to keep Daisy's powerful claws and teeth away from his flesh by further use of his jacket, but there was no hope of taming him and in no time at all he escaped and returned to the wild.

We were worried about Daisy and asked Dad if he couldn't try to catch him again.

"No," was his reply, "when a cat goes wild like that and grows huge by feeding on fat rabbits, he'll never tame again."

So we had to be content to have known Daisy in happier days. Mind you, Daisy probably figured himself to be pretty happy right then, keeping down on the rabbit population and lazing in the summer sun ... in retrospect, it is not surprising that he went wild, not with the name we gave him.

I recall one day some boys were down at the beach and caught a plucker (sea scorpion: *cottus bubalis*). They decided to take the prickly fellow and have some fun by 'smoking the plucker on a peat'. This was done by placing the living fish on a peat, putting a straw in its mouth and lighting the end. The fish would then draw the smoke in and puff it out again.

I had seen this done before and at first had thought it was great fun, but I soon realised how much suffering this caused the fish and was always glad when it was returned to the sea.

We were soon on the move again and left the lovely shores of Westsandwick with some regret, to return to Mid Yell to live for a while in the little house at Ravensgeo, with Daa, Granny Katie, Uncle John and aunts Annie, Bertha and Mary.

It was really a case of sardines in tins at bedtime when we bairns often slept in a bed made up on the 'ben' room floor. However, it was warm and comfortable and we were happy to have so many loving people around us.

We were back at our old school again and of one thing we were sure, when we were allowed out at the end of the school day we would find our grandfather waiting for us. Daa rarely missed a day and, unless there was something special on, he would be there waiting to walk back home with us and our friends, Sylvia and Ethel, who lived near us in Ravensgeo. He was a warm-hearted man who loved children, but he also knew that if he was with us we arrived home much sooner than we might have done.

Yet, as much as we enjoyed being with them all, the situation could not continue and presently Dad found a job on Culsetter farm in the south of mainland Shetland. Almost before we knew it we were saying a fond farewell to Yell and all our friends there.

Living on a farm was a new experience for us. There were new interests, such as 'helping' Dad in the hay fields or in the barn or the byre, where there seemed to be an air of contentment as he did the milking. I would stand there sometimes just listening to the sounds of the place: now and then a cow would snort or breathe heavily, stamp a foot impatiently as it waited to be milked; then there was a lazy swishing of tails and the sound of milk splashing into the pail. The smells, too, gave the place a feeling of magic, the animal foods and newly cut hay were a never-to-be-forgotten part of that farm.

I'll always remember how delighted the cattle were to be allowed out in the spring. I'd never seen such large animals jumping in the air and kicking up their heels like lambs.

Then we received the news that Grandfather John Strachan had died, on the 30th March, 1950. I had not known him as well as I had my mother's father, but we were all saddened by the news. It was the first time I'd ever seen tears in Dad's eyes and that shocked me more than anything else.

Once, when we'd been to a party, Hamish decided to go with the van running some of his pals home, whilst the rest of us walked back along the road to the farm. He was sorry later that he had gone for the run as the van went over a bump in the road, the door flew open and he fell out. There were no seat belts in those days and he was the unlucky boy who sat next to the door. He swore later that the back wheel went over his knee, but luckily no bones were broken though his knee was badly cut.

We spent many hours of play in, or beside, the Burn of Hillwell. There were small trout in the burn and we made many attempts to catch some, but they always seemed to avoid us. On several occasions we tried, unsuccessfully, to tickle (guddle) them out of the water. If we were lucky enough to catch any our aim was not to kill or eat them, but to return them to a dammed-up area where they were supposed to stay and grow fat as 'tame' fish ... this early attempt at fish farming was doomed to failure as our dam was not well built and the fish escaped in a few minutes.

One of the finest things that happened there was that Sheila came into our lives. She was a border collie/whippet cross and was born at Culsetter that spring. It was very likely our pleading that persuaded Dad to keep one of the puppies for us.

At that stage we didn't know that we were soon to leave there to settle for several years in a place that was a perfect playground for children ... East Shore, Virkie.

Chapter Five

Stories

I kicked moodily at a stone on the dusty road and trudged slowly on. It was a lovely sunny morning and I disliked the idea of sitting in school when, deep in my heart, I yearned to be running along the sand or searching for crabs in a rock pool.

From some distance ahead Rose and her companions called to me to hurry up or I would be late and get into trouble. At the thought of maybe getting the strap I regretfully put my yearnings aside and ran to join them.

Dad was now employed on Sumburgh farm and we lived in a little house in East Shore, Virkie. It was a splendid place for children as the house was situated by the large, almost circular, area of sand and sea, called the Pool of Virkie. When the tide was out there was only a narrow channel of water called the 'Trinky' running from the mouth of the Pool to an inner area of water near the south-western shore, leaving the rest pure sand which was ideal for playing bare-foot games on. Even when the tide was in the water was not terribly deep and we often waded around up to our knees in the clear water.

All that day I was inattentive, my eyes often on the patch of blue sky I could see through the window. I was reprimanded several times by our eagle-eyed teacher who was not one to allow slacking in her class.

Playtime and dinnertime were breaks in the monotony of school life, but seemed so very short. Once back in the class time seemed to move even more slowly and soon the sky outside was dark and lowering ... it began to look as if our good spell of weather was over.

I doubt if I was the first one out of school that day but I certainly wasn't the last. My heart sank as raindrops pattered down on my head.

Isn't it strange how children seem to hurry home light-heartedly on sunny days, but at the first few raindrops, appear to go into slow motion. That day Rose and I covered the distance to our little home with foot-dragging slowness, even pausing to splash our feet in puddles on the road that had been dusty dry in the morning.

"I hate school," I told Rose, kicking my foot through a puddle and gasping a little as the cold wetness splashed up under my short pants. "I don't see why bairns have to learn so much."

"I just hate one teacher," Rose replied with feeling. "I'll always mind how she mocked me when I said words the Yell way. She made me stand in front o' the class an' read. Then, when I said words the Yell way everybody laughed."

Which just goes to show the prejudice that was between the dialects of different islands and the mental cruelty meted out by some teachers in those days.

"Never mind," I said, "this is Friday so we'll have the weekend free."

"Are we goin' to Lerwick tomorrow?" she asked.

We sometimes took the bus up to town on Saturday, which meant we had a day out as the bus only returned in the early evening. I was never sure whether I liked the bustle of town or not. There were far too many people and noisy vehicles in it for my liking and I often wondered how folk could bear to live there with so many large buildings around them.

Now I said to Rose, "I dunno. Maybe."

She was silent as we walked up around the corner and onto the path leading to our door. Then she said, "I'll ask Mum."

We were met at the door by an excitable, but nervous Sheila, who was obviously delighted by our return, but apprehensive too ... children in her life were strange creatures who might pet her one moment and tease her the next. We'd found an ideal method of keeping her off chairs: an old rubber hot-water bottle with a hole in it placed under a cushion made a noise that frightened her into jumping down ... no wonder she was a bundle of nerves! Mind you, should we forget and leave the bottle on the chair, and unexpectedly be visited by a neighbour, or even the minister, there could be a few

Rose and John Arnold with Sheila in East Shore Virkie.

embarrassing moments all round and our 'black affronted' mother would give us a good telling off after the equally affronted visitor had departed.

Sheila was not our only animal friend as we had acquired two Dutch rabbits and Louise, a pure white kitten. She had been given one of Princess Anne's names as she was born on the same day.

When we'd fought off our face-licking welcome committee we entered the house, turning left into the 'but' end which served as kitchen, living room and workroom, where Mum was busy with something on the table inside the window where the light could fall on her work.

"Oh, my peerie bairns, are you soakin'?" she greeted us, hastening to feel our wet clothes. "Tak' you yon wet things off. You're surely no' been playin' out in the rain? Why, I saw the Garrick bairns goin' by ages ago, I don't know what you were thinkin' about."

Perhaps we were wise to remain silent at this point in time. I wanted to go out and play on the beach, rain or not, but I knew what the answer to that would be so I just removed my wet jacket which she took to hang on the back of a chair. Then, opening the doors of the stove wide, she placed the chair where the heat from the peaty embers could do their work and dry the jacket and Rose's wet coat, which was hanging nearby.

Sheila jumped up in the armchair just as I went towards it with the intention of sitting. I glared at her, as settling down she grinned up at me showing a full set of fine white teeth, before burrowing her nose under the cushion and rolling one eye as if to say she'd beat me to it ... things were not going well for me this day!

She could be so amusing at times and I changed my mind and turned to go ben, thinking to myself that next time she tried that she'd find a very noisy hot-water bottle under the cushion.

The house had only three rooms. The ben room was almost the same size as the but end, whilst the third was much smaller and stood between them, and was lit by a small window in the back wall.

The most memorable thing about the ben end was that its walls were a nauseous blue, faded in places so that the whole room looked as if some mad artist had splashed the colour on the walls then tried to wash it off again.

This was also our bedroom where I now went in search of something to do. As often as not I would have played some games with Rose but I wasn't in the mood, and anyway, she was now intent on 'helping' Mum with whatever she was doing in the but end.

Walking into the ben room I saw the books lying on a chair beside the bed and picked them up. They were 'Whip Hand' by Walter Rhoades, and 'Arabian Nights'. I opened 'Whip Hand' and read what was written on the flyleaf. The book had been a special prize for drawing from Westsandwick school in Yell. It was dated June 1949 and signed by the teacher Annie M. Leask. I'd just finished reading it again so I laid it down and picked up 'Arabian Nights'.

It had never been my wish to attend any school, but there was a certain thrill about seeing my name written on the flyleaf. Even at that age books fascinated me. It was not that I was a good reader, or a fast one, but there was something about them that set my heart beating faster and the ones I'd been given at school were special. I might not like school but I did enjoy the books they gave as prizes.

In no time at all I settled down on the bed and began to read. I was in a wonderland of strange people and exotic places when Rose came to see if I wanted anything to eat or drink. Mum was making herself a cup of tea and we could have something too if we wished.

Hamish was at Sandwick Secondary School, a few miles further up the coast, which involved a journey in a school bus, so he wouldn't be in for some time yet.

I had a drink of tea and a biscuit with Mum and Rose and returned to my book. I was so deep in the tales of the east that I failed to hear Hamish come in until I became aware that someone had entered the room, spoken to me, and gone out again.

I hurried through to see who it was and as I came out of the room I heard Hamish ask, "Is John Arnold in a bad mood, for I just spoke ta him an' he never answered?"

"I was readin'," I said, before anyone else could speak, "I didna hear what you said."

"More likely sleepin'," Hamish grinned.

I ignored his comment and walked over to where Rose was knitting, or trying to.

"I could do that," I said, forgetting for the moment that my last attempt had ended in failure.

Rose didn't even glance at me, such was her concentration, but Hamish laughed and said, "Yea, we know what your makkin is like. Mind the time you started makkin a gansey an' it just turned out like a long, thin tie, an' you got mad when we laughed, an' never tried again?"

I was rather ashamed of my first attempt at knitting, mainly because nearly everyone in the islands could knit, including our parents, who, from as far back as I remember had worked with knitting (makkin) machines. In those days when women went visiting about an evening they would take their knitting with them. When inviting a woman to visit them they would say: "Come along ... an tak dee makkin." A saying now sadly gone out of use.

I resented Hamish's comments and sulked my way back to my book.

"You needna sulk, for what I've said is true," Hamish called after me. Then, to Mum, "Well, if he wasna in a bad mood before, he surely is now."

"Oh, leave him alone," she ordered. "You know he can't help that he can't makk. There's a lot o' folk that never manage it right."

If I had really thought about it I would have realised that the only reason I could not knit was that I had so little interest in it. In fact, I would rather have read a book any day. I had not, at that age, been visited by the idea that if I could read a story I could also write one. It would be just over two years before that amazing piece of intelligence burst its way into my mind, and another forty-two before I got around to writing anything worth printing.

I stayed curled up on the bed reading until Dad came home. Then he came ben, obviously having been told that I was in severe sulkulation.

"Boy," he said, with a laugh in his voice and a twinkle in his eyes, "is this whaur you are?"

"I'm just readin'," I said.

"Eh, readin'." He raised an eyebrow at me, "I heard you were in a terrible temper."

"No. Well, it was just Hamish mockin' my makkin, an I couldna help that my gansey turned oot lookin' more lik' a tie."

"What? But, John Arnold," he seemed to be surprised, "that was years ago. Why, I'll bet if you tried it now you'd pick it up no bother."

"I don't really want to," I replied, "I'd rather read a book."

"Well, that's fine," he said. Dad was not a great reader, yet I felt he understood.

"It's never easy to be the only one in a family who can't do something," he said. "I mind when I was a boy my six older brothers could all swim, but I couldn't. I felt terrible about it, but I thought they would laugh at me if I asked them to teach me, so I found a length of rope and went down to the seashore and tied each end to a rock. I was away out of sight of anyone and hadn't realised the dangers. Anyway, I got into the water and, holding onto the rope, began learning myself to swim." He paused, his eyes looking away back into the past as he relived that experience.

"What happened?" I asked.

"Well, I made two or three journeys along the rope between the rocks, holding on with one hand and kicking my legs and splashing with my free hand, before I lost my grip on it and began to sink down into the deep water. I knew I was in trouble for there was no one to come to my rescue and as far as I knew I was alone. Struggling desperately I tried to keep my head above water and find the rope at the same time.

"Suddenly, there was a splash beside me and stronger arms than mine grasped hold of me and pulled me out. Spluttering an' choking I looked up into the face of another Vatsetter lad, Tammie

John and Helen Strachan, our grandparents. Vatsetter, c.1940s.

The S.S. Anthea, rammed and sunk in convoy HX.93, 1940.

Leask. He had seen me with the rope and followed to see what I was up to ... and lucky for me he did so, too."

"But you can swim now, Dad?"

"Yea, after that I learned well enough," for a moment he looked sternly at me, then grinned and added, "so, if there's something you need to learn don't be afraid to ask for there's always some kind-hearted soul ready to teach you. Come now, we'd best go through, the tea'll be about ready."

We sometimes persuaded Dad to tell us about his adventures in the merchant navy and that evening was no exception, for as soon as tea was over, Hamish began asking once more about the sinking of the S.S. *Anthea* in 1940, and with a sigh of resignation and a few extra strong puffs on his pipe he began: "Well, the S.S. *Anthea* was built in 1924 by Ardrossan Dockyard and Shipbuilding Company for C.T. Bowering Steamship Company of London. After I joined her she was sent out to Canada an' for some time we sailed about out there. This was in 1940 an' we'd been at war for about a year, so ships crossing the Atlantic went in convoy in an effort to prevent lone vessels from being sunk by German U-boats. So, when we were ready to return to Britain, the *Anthea* joined convoy HX.93 and we all set out for home

"Now, the convoy speed was set at ten knots and that was about as fast as the poor old *Anthea* could go, so she was having some difficulty keeping up with the others."

"What was her cargo?" Hamish asked.

"Well, there was grain, army trucks and some of the finest motor-cars you could see."

"There were eight other Yell men on her," Hamish said, "weren't there?"

"Yes, including James John, your cousin."

We all knew this already but it was good to get all the details again. James John's father, Jamie, lived just along the road from us having settled down in Virkie.

"Well," Dad continued, "on the 8th December we were travelling without lights, according to wartime regulations, an' the night was as black as pitch. Most o' the crew, including myself, were in the fo'c'sle sleeping, but three of the Yell men were on watch – Peter Walker, Sonny Slater and Peter Goodlad who was on the wheel.

"Then, just before three o'clock in the morning the Dutch liner *Maasdam* suddenly came surging through the waves, her bow aimed straight for the *Anthea's* side. There was nothing anyone could do, an' the first I knew about it was when I was rudely awakened by the shock of the collision and things being thrown about, lik' the stove that was sent right across the cabin.

"We were lucky that our bunks were all in the centre of the fo'c'sle or someone could have been badly injured or killed. We found that the lockers had been overturned and we were trapped in the fo'c'sle by the twisted and buckled steel plates and other wreckage that blocked the door."

"What did you do?" I asked.

"Well, John Arnold," he smiled at me, "we were seven desperate seamen I can tell you, but we managed to climb out through the gaping hole left by the bow of the *Maasdam* and get to the dubious safety of the deck. We were just in time too, for as we

The Yell survivors of the S.S. Anthea. Back: Peter Walker, Robert Guthrie, Dan Spence, Andrew Spence, Gerry Brown. Front: James John Strachan, Peter Goodlad, Sonny Slater and Tammie Strachan.

climbed out the sea rushed in with some force and in seconds the bow deck was almost at the water line. Just after that the captain gave the order to abandon ship."

"It must have been terrible feeling locked in," Hamish said.

"Aye," Dad agreed, "we were glad to be out, though it wasn't so fine in the life boat, but eventually we were picked up by the *Maasdam* and taken to Halifax where we were treated very kindly."

"How did you get back home?" Hamish asked.

"Well, we should have come back on a ship called the *Western Chief* but plans were changed and we returned on the *Anacortes*. We were lucky there too for the *Western Chief* was torpedoed in mid-Atlantic and sunk.

"I can tell you this boys, I never want to have a trip lik' that again. Oh, the old *Anacortes* was a fine enough ship, but we joined a twenty-four-ship convoy an' just when we were beginning to think we might make port without U-boat trouble they found us. It was about five hundred miles west of Ireland and out of twenty-four ships only six made it safely to port."

Dad and his six older brothers had all been merchant seamen, and once, so the story goes, they were all on the same vessel. We would have loved to have asked him to tell a lot more stories about his past adventures but there were things he and our mother had to do if we were to go to town in the morning. Aye, in those days a day in town meant dressing-up in your best attire, so there was a lot to be done.

Most important, however, was our hair. Hair cutting was something we boys did not care for, but with Dad doing the job we didn't object.

Once he said in exasperation, "How can you cut this boy's hair? For it goes in every direction under the sun." I made no reply for as he spoke the hand-operated hair-cutters were travelling up the back of my neck and I sat very still.

Presently we were done and, feeling as if we had been scalped, we sat with silly grins on our faces until told to move ourselves out of the way.

We were so excited that we could hardly get to sleep that night, but at last our eyes shut in slumber and then it was morning and we were being urged to get out of bed.

Chapter Six

The Egg Hunter's Mistake

Soon we were walking up the road by the shop to where we caught the bus. Often there were several other people waiting there and they would greet our parents by name: "Hello Tammie. Hello Georgina. We should have a fine run ta town this mornin'."

Usually there would just be a few comments on the weather or some item of local interest.

"Hit'll rain later on noo that the wind has gone ta the sooth wast," some weather dependent old crofter might say. Or a woman would comment to our mother, "We had a lovely time at the hall last night, such a pity you missed it. Oh, that reminds me ... " and she would go on to some news of interest concerning the district.

Hanging around just waiting bored me, and that morning I kicked idly at a stone, which narrowly missed Hamish's leg. I hadn't kicked it at him, but just because it was lying there at the toe of my shoe. However, my thoughtless move had been seen and my father said sharply, "John Arnold, behave, or you'll be in trouble."

'Trouble' from Dad meant a good stiff talking-to. I can't ever recall him raising his hand to any of us, but he had enough authority in a look to make us toe the line.

"What's John Arnold done, Mummy?" Rose asked, only to be answered by a "Shush now, watch for the bus coming."

There were other people at the stop that morning so I just hung my head in embarrassment and turned away from all the staring eyes.

I was glad when the bus came and we could disappear into our seats, away from adult eyes. I was always interested in what lay outside the bus windows as we journeyed along.

There were occasional scattered villages, and more distant houses. Some crofts were close to the road and there was always

Our mother, Georgina Leask in the 1930s.

someone waving a cheery greeting to the driver and his passengers. Sometimes, too, the bus would stop to allow more people to embark, and now and then, waiting at some lonely road end, would be a solitary figure carrying a box or bag, who would give his burden to the driver with instructions as to where it was to be left in town.

On the bus adult conversation was usually concerned with the weather, crops, livestock, fishing and knitwear. Undoubtedly there were other subjects, as the Shetland crofters of those days were great readers and were very knowledgeable on many subjects.

At last, however, we arrived in Lerwick and after disembarking we walked in over 'The Street'. At that time Commercial Street was the main shopping centre, there being no big stores elsewhere, in or outside the town, as there are today.

We children often pleaded to be taken to shops selling toys or sweeties and were sometimes given that treat. One day Rose was in serious trouble when she dropped some little bauble, which shattered, and Mum had to pay for it. Thereafter we were warned never to pick up things in shops. These were hard times and our parents' finances really couldn't stretch to breakages, or the expensive toys we desired, but there was always some little thing that pleased. (What the children of today, with a seemingly endless supply of toys, would think if they could be transported back to the 1950s I don't know, but I bet I know which were the more contented.)

I was never sure if I liked being in town or not, for it seemed so alien when compared to our simple way of life. Here, there were no green fields, and the only flowers we saw were stuck in a bucket outside a shop doorway. Then, when we did manage to see the sea in the harbour, it was cold grey-blue water lapping angrily at the quayside, not the bluer, much more friendly, waters of the Pool.

By the end of the afternoon we were beginning to tire with being unaccustomed to walking on the hard streets. Feet that were often running bare on soft sand did not enjoy being trapped in hard shoes on concrete.

We had enjoyed our visit to a restaurant, and possibly eaten too much, but being in such a place had reminded us of a story we'd been told:

One day, many years ago, two old crofter brothers who rarely left their home travelled to Lerwick and, after shopping for a while entered a restaurant for a meal. Food was soon placed before them and they began to eat. Then one of them spied a dish filled with a yellow substance not unlike the custard they sometimes made at home. Ever ready for a new culinary experience he spooned some of it onto his plate and from there into his mouth.

Suddenly he gasped and, clasping his throat, struggled to get to his feet but instead began to sink towards the floor.

Duncan, the other brother, was soon on his feet shouting, "Poison! Poison!"

The restaurateur and his staff were soon on the scene, alarmed by such cries, which were extremely bad for business.

"He ate some o' yon yellow stuff an' choked," Duncan was quick to explain.

"But," wailed the restaurateur, "that is mustard. You only eat a little of it mixed in with your food … never by the spoonful."

Duncan looked at the people around him before, with dramatically pointing finger, he cried, "Be it mouse dirt or cat's dirt, Donald is dead … and there he lies."

Of course, Donald was not dead, and after being given water to drink he revived well enough to half-heartedly finish his dinner … but it is very doubtful if he ever tried to eat mustard again.

Long bus journeys tended to make me drowsy so I was in a sort of half stupor before the bus had gone far on our way home.

The next day being Sunday meant us being trapped indoors again for a little while as we attended Virkie Sabbath School. I liked that school as much as I liked any other school, but at least it did not last as long as day school.

As the year wore on and the nights became darker we still were allowed to play outside for a few hours in the evening … and what fun we had. A small weight, a drawing pin and a long length of thread meant that we could rig up a 'tappie' on someone's door. People inside would hear a tapping sound at the door, but on opening found no one there.

Either that, or one of us would creep up to the door, knock

loudly, then run away and hide. These and other tricks we played were harmless, if annoying, to our patient neighbours. Only once or twice did one of them actually come out and give chase. One dark night she shone her 'blinky' (torch) out over the rigs to find us, not knowing that at least two of us could have reached out and touched her toes. Every now and then the distant lighthouse on Sumburgh Head would flash our way and we would hug the earth in case its beam gave away our position. As it was, we were lying perilously close to a large bunch of nettles.

A daytime game often included that clump of nettles when it was at its best in summer. The idea was that each of us tried to jump over the clump, and if you failed to cover the distance, or otherwise miscalculated your jump, your bare legs and arms were severely stung ... one of those silly games boys dream up. You wouldn't catch girls doing that ... or would you?

We used the lighthouse too, in a game in which the aim was to move only in the dark space of time between flashes. Anyone still moving when the light shone our way lost the game.

We also raided crops, especially around Hallowe'en, when we needed the big swede turnip for a 'neepie lantern'. Aye, and we had some fun trying to hollow them out properly. Of course, we did occasionally take one just to eat raw in our little gang-hut, which was a stone, roofed shed built onto the end of the house, or rather, onto the end of the shed proper which adjoined the house and in which Dad worked at various things, including the building of model yachts.

Our night-time adventures, annoying as they might have been to our neighbours, were nothing compared to the tricks played in our parents' day. I recall my mother telling about a time when she and her companions were playing tricks in Mid Yell.

"One of the boys," she explained, "took a peat from the stack and climbed up on the roof of the house in order to lay it on the top of the lum can. We all hid behind the stack and waited to see what would happen. Suddenly the door banged open and the man came out, followed by several billows of peat reek. We watched in silence as the man, the only occupant, stepped away from the house to look up at the lum. Well, he started shouting and swearing when he saw the peat and we figured it was time to get out of there as he might be violent.

"So, we broke cover and ran for it but he wasna goin' to be outdone by us and as soon as he saw us he came after us at the run. That was a fright! I was the last one and he was gaining fast as we raced down over the braes. I really thought he was goin' to catch me, but I was lucky and we all got away."

Putting a peat or turf on top of a chimney pot seems to have been a widely used trick in Shetland in times past, but what was really nasty was for the tricksters to tie the door handle too so that the inhabitants could only get out with difficulty.

Another trick was to paint the window glass so that the sleeping people inside could not tell when day dawned. This trick was not often used and was not very successful if only one window was treated in this way.

Dad, his brothers and friends, also played a great many tricks and once took a rowing boat from the Linkshouse beach on the south side of Mid Yell, rowed it across to the north side, pulled it up on the beach at Seafield and left it there. They had not been seen and walked around the voe to await the results.

The boat's owner missed his vessel but had no idea where it was so couldn't fetch it. However, a couple of days later the local police constable, Charlie Gray, tapped Dad on the shoulder and said sternly, "Tammie, just take your pals an' go around and fetch yon boat back. Yes, right back whaur you took her from."

Dad acted the innocent, but only for a moment.

"Now, Tammie, I'm givin' you fair warning. Stop playing tricks like yon," Charlie said, "or you'll all be in a lot of trouble. Mind, if you don't stop I'll have to take action."

They might not have been seen moving the boat, but Charlie had his finger on the pulse of the village and knew very well who the tricksters were.

We played many games on the sand when the tide was out. Sometimes there was only the three of us, but we were often joined by other friends such as the Garrick girls who lived along the road from us, and there were days when there was a larger gathering of us

Georgina Leask with Vina Gray, c.1930s.

on the sand. Then the air would resound with our excited cries and the thwack of ball on bat.

As the year drew to a close I was surprised to be given a prize for class work from Virkie Sabbath School ... another book, 'The Young Rankins' by H. M. MacLeod. I was delighted.

Even in those days when times were hard, Christmas seemed to have a special kind of magic about it, even if Santa didn't bring many toys, and never as many as we asked for in the letters we posted up the lum. There was always something nice though, some fruit, a few sweeties, toy vehicles for us boys and maybe a doll or so for Rose. Dad was very good with his hands and would make us some little thing to help the Santa collection. Then there would be the odd board game such as snakes and ladders or ludo, and once a wooden monkey on a stick. How we loved making him climb to the top. All in all Christmas Day was a very joyful time.

The road came down by the end of the house and then branched to the east and west. It ran along Eastshore for some distance, but stopped at the last house. The westward branch ran by the cottages where Uncle Jamie Strachan stayed, continuing on to the airport and the village of Toab where our school was.

Just below where the three roads met was the 'Dump' – a heap of earth, over which many items were dumped. Once we found many tins of wartime dried milk, which had obviously been dumped out of a shop, and they ended up in our shed where we sampled some of it dry. I suppose our idea was, that if it was good enough for children during the war it was good enough for us, some five or six years later.

Then spring came and with it my eleventh birthday. How I wished boys of that age did not have to go to school each day, but I knew that no matter how much I pleaded that case I was bound to lose. So, reluctantly and with toe-dragging slowness I would set out for school every morning with Rose.

There were compensations, however, as sometimes we would see some unusual bird, or a plane would be taking off or landing at the airport. In the cornfields between us and the cottages we would sometimes see or hear a corncrake. This bird was once widespread in the islands, but due to the change in land use, has declined seriously. During my childhood there were enough small crofts growing grain crops to encourage corncrakes to nest.

In those days bird-nesting was something little boys did from time to time. One evening in spring, Hamish decided that we would go out bird-nesting.

"We'll go to the Point o' Tangpool, or maybe up towards The Taing," Hamish said. "We might even get as far as Millburn Geo. There's sure to be lots of nests out that way."

I nodded in agreement, but Mum overhead and now said sternly, "I don't want you, or John Arnold, climbing in the banks, Hamish. I tink yon's a silly idea."

"We'll no' be climbing in any cliffs," he replied, "for the birds nest all over the ground an' it's no' a silly idea ... it's the only way I'll ever get any decent eggs."

"I wish you'd collect something sensible," says she, "an' not go putting yourselves in danger."

"Ach," Hamish was on the point of open rebellion, "there's no danger an' I promise no' ta let John Arnold go near the banks."

"It's okay, Mum," I said, "we'll no' be long, Well, just long enough ta get an egg or two."

In the end she reluctantly allowed us to go as long as we promised to keep away from the cliffs.

So we hurried through Eastshore, going along the beach for a bit, before moving up onto the grassy area of Brough Head. Here could be seen the remains of an ancient broch, but I doubt if we even gave it a second glance as we went eagerly on our way. At last we reached the point of Tangpool and began to walk north along the top of the cliffs, keeping a lookout for nests on the ground as we went.

We soon knew when we were nearing the nesting birds for they began to mob us. Seagulls by the dozen nested in this area and they did not welcome little boys on egg-hunting trips.

Soon Hamish found a nest with several eggs in it and took one, went to another nest nearby and took another. Gently he slipped them into his jacket pocket, found another couple and dropped them into his other pocket. Then we headed for home, but eggs are fragile things and we had a long way to go.

When we arrived at the house there was a certain strong smell following Hamish, and it was with something akin to horror that he discovered that an egg in his right hand pocket had broken and was completely rotten.

His face was a sight to see as he pulled his rot-covered fingers out of his pocket.

"Yaach!" he cried, "it's rotten! It must'a' been there for ages ... oh, what a stink!"

Our mother's disgusted face would have told any watcher just what she thought when she learned about the egg-hunter's mistake. She left him in no doubt as to what she thought about "This egg-collecting nonsense".

Hamish groaned as he began to slowly remove his odoriferous jacket ... things were not going his way and that was sure.

Not long after we came to Eastshore we found an enamelled tray, which must have been part of a cover for some engine or heater that became very hot, for on the back there were five places where the enamel had been removed by someone placing their fingertips on the hot tray ... no doubt a painful experience. That tray became a very useful item on our indoor playing scene. We would spread our toys on it, and once it became a Plasticine city called 'Elatchton'. So, the tray that gave one person much agony also gave some children a great deal of enjoyment.

Another book came my way as a prize from Virkie Public School. This was 'The Stolen Trophy' by W. Kersley Holmes, a very enjoyable read for an eleven-year-old boy.

One book we'd had for years was 'Out With Garibaldi'. It belonged to Hamish but I read and reread it, slowly, but with much delight. I also read and enjoyed 'Submarine Alone' by Hackforth-Jones and 'The Black Dragon' by John Sylvester. My love of books did not prevent me from reading comics and the 'Dandy', 'Beano' and 'Topper' were great favourites, as were 'Oor Wullie' and the 'Broons'. We also loved the series in the 'Weekly News' called "Black Bob", about a shepherd and his faithful friend.

The holiday season came around again and we were delighted when we learned that we were going to spend some of the holidays in Mid Yell with Daa, Granny Katie, the aunts and Uncle John Leask. It would be lovely to see them again, so we were soon counting the days until the school broke up for the summer holidays.

Chapter Seven

Return to Yell

At last the day came when we set out for Yell, first catching the bus to Lerwick, and later in the day, boarding another bus which took us up to the ferry at Toft. No roll-on roll-off ferries in those days, but a little motorboat to take us across Yell Sound to Ulsta in Yell.

We always liked to stand out on deck with the men, but often spray from the bows went the length of the vessel so we were usually ordered below. I didn't like being stuck in the cabin with a group of inquisitive women, but often there was nothing to do but grin and bear it. Sometimes there were days when the weather was not so good and even the hardiest of men sought the shelter of the little cabin.

This time, however, the trip wasn't too bad and we were soon clambering ashore on Yell. There, waiting for us, was the bus and its cheerful driver, who would take us north along East Yell to our destination.

Old Daa was always ready and waiting long before the appointed time and would have been at the bus stop for about thirty minutes before we arrived. He was a stoutish man with a big moustache, not tall but very strong. A good-humoured man who enjoyed a good laugh and a yarn. He liked a hand of cards about an evening, or a game of draughts.

One of the best things about our holidays with Daa and Granny was the fact that Daa had a boat. She was a typical Shetland foureareen (four-oared) held together with tar that had been coated on her sides to seal any leaks rather than to make her look good. I doubt if even Daa knew just how old she was, but she must have been well up amongst the senior citizens of the rowing boat world.

As we came up the road from Linkshouse we saw two figures waiting by the hall and recognised Daa and Uncle John. When the

Daa and Granny Katie; Andrew and Catherine Leask.

bus stopped and we disembarked I felt like dancing a jig of delight, but I was far too shy for any such display of wild emotion.

After greeting us Daa and John vied for the doubtful pleasure of carrying our heaviest belongings down the road to the little house we knew so well.

As we passed Brown's Garage we heard voices but no one came out so we continued on our way. This was the garage to which we were sent when the radio accumulator required recharging. The Brown brothers were cheerful company, and if I was about bursting with shyness when I entered the building I was much less so by the time I left, for the good natured banter soon put you at your ease.

So we went on our way until we came abreast of the little house in which we had spent time some years before.

"Mummy," Rose said, looking at the little building, "I'll have to go and visit Anderina."

The Yell Sound ferry arrives at Ulsta pier.

"We'll go later," was the reply, "when we've rested for a bit."

"All right," Rose agreed, "but I'd like to go as soon as possible."

She sounded as if this visit was extremely important to her and I suppose it was as she had not seen the old lady for about a year.

From there we were going downhill passing, on the right side, the larger house in which Tom Brown and his family lived. To the left of us was the cottage in which the Browns who had Brown's shop lived. The shop stood just a few yards down but on the right side of the road. As we went by this cottage there came a furious barking from their dog. If I remember correctly this was a Scotch terrier.

Daa led the way down the brae by the shop. Then we bairns ran on ahead, eager to get down to the peerie house at Ravensgeo. As we turned the corner, just beyond Karl Anderson's garages, we glanced back and saw that our folks had stopped briefly to speak to someone at the garage door, so we paused and waited for them to come on again.

The road we'd come down continued on to Gardiestaing, but we now journeyed along the Ravensgeo branch and soon came in sight of our holiday abode. Granny Katie and our aunts were waiting to give us a warm welcome, and to me it felt as if I'd come home again ... and I suppose I had.

The first thing we wanted to do was to get out and visit all our favourite haunts; go down to the beach and check that Daa's old boat was still seaworthy; that the sillocks still swam by the hundred around the old pier; that there was still water in the peerie pond up behind the house. After such a long time away we often had to improve the dam, which meant throwing some more mud onto the place where the tiny stream ran from the pond. It was not much of a stream, little more than a trickle, but after some work the pond soon filled again.

Water beetles and other insect life also loved the pond, which is possibly why none of our tadpoles seemed to survive as water beetles and their larvae would have made short work of them.

A day or two after our arrival we heard the knock-knock sound of an engine coming into the voe. Norwegian fishing boat engines were unmistakable and we were all excited at the prospect of a visit from them.

We all knew the story of the 'Shetland Bus' when those courageous Norwegian fishermen dared the might of Hitler's Germany to aid their people and the Allies in their little wooden boats.

I don't know the names of those who visited Mid Yell, nor do I recall the names of their boats, but they were always welcomed warmly. If there was some function on, such as a concert and dance, then they would be eager to join in. First, though, they would have to visit one of the shops in the island, licensed to sell alcohol. This meant a car, or some vehicle, would need to be organised to take them there and bring them back. It wouldn't be long before this was done, and some of the local lads would accompany them ... very likely a good time was had by all. Whatever, we young-uns would be in dreamland long before they returned.

It was not only Norwegian boats that visited Mid Yell and there would often be trawlers from the east coast of Scotland, or further south. Many of those who visited the house in Ravensgeo spoke the same Doric tongue as had Grandfather Strachan, so was not all that strange to us.

When the trawlers came into the voe, Daa would get his boat

into the water and he and Uncle John would row off to the anchored vessel and invite them to come ashore.

Once, between the wars, such a vessel came to anchor there and the trawler's men were only too pleased to use Daa's boat to ferry themselves ashore. After an enjoyable time somewhere Daa rowed them back to their vessel.

One of the men asked Daa's name, and on being told Andrew Leask said, "Oh, I was in prison camp with a George Leask from Mid Yell."

Anderina Inkster and Jean Ratter, Reafirth, Mid Yell.

"That was my brother George," Daa replied in some surprise.

Up until that moment none of the family had known more than that George (or Dodie as he was known in the family) had died in a German prison camp during the First World War. Now Daa was to find out what really happened.

George was the strongest of the family and was reputed to be powerful enough to break out of handcuffs and do other feats of strength. Then came the war, which saw him captured and taken prisoner. The Germans soon realised his power and decided to use him as a guinea pig. Thereafter, he was infected by a variety of diseases as his captors attempted to find a cure for such scourges of mankind as diphtheria, typhoid, smallpox and cholera. Sadly, even George's mighty strength was unable to fight off this adversary and he perished.

This story must have come as a shock to Daa and perhaps that is why he kept the story to himself for many years and only broke silence about it to my father not long before his death. It may be that his reason for not spreading the story was a wish not to upset other members of his family.

Many times when visitors called the evening would be spent in the but end yarning or telling stories from around the islands. Granny Katie and the aunts kept everyone well supplied with cups of tea and biscuits, and if we were very lucky, a round, thick oatmeal brünnie.

I loved to listen to them as the stories flew back and forth, each seeming to try to outdo the other. Unfortunately my memory has retained only a few of these stories, helped, perhaps, by hearing them again in more recent years.

"My father," said one of the visitors, "used to tell the story o' the *Carmelan*, a Dutch ship that was bound for the East Indies in the year 1664, which came to grief on the rocks at Skerries … "

"Yea," commented Daa, "I mind hearin' about her. Did she no' have a fairly rich cargo?"

"That she did. They say her cargo was worth three or four million pound. Aye, an' that it was in gold bullion and a great number o' chests crammed fu' wi' gold coins." He paused to draw on his pipe as the firelight flickered over his rugged features.

Then he continued, "It was a very dark night and nothing could be seen of any land ahead, but they were sure that the islands were near so they sent four men up into the rigging as lookouts, but even they didna see the low lyin' islands in time and she ran full tilt on to the jagged rocks," again he paused, this time to take the pipe out of his mouth and hold it like a pointer in his hand.

"Now see," he said, wagging the pipe stem at his listeners as if to emphasise the story, "when she struck, one or more of her masts broke off and fell on to the cliffs. Aye, and it was in that way the four men posted in the rigging managed to scramble ashore and be saved, but the rest o' the crew were lost."

"Yea," said another visitor, "but what happened ta aa that gold?"

"Ach," the storyteller replied, "as far as I know it's still there for 'tis said she drifted off an' sank in deep watter."

"John Arnold," said Granny Katie, "would you go and pump up the Tilley lamp?"

I needed no second bidding for I enjoyed pumping the lamp when the pressure began to ail and the room darkened. After a few pumps the firelight on folks' faces seemed to fade away as the lamp brightened ... a good Tilley was as good as electric light any day and much more interesting.

When I returned to my seat Daa was saying, "That minds me o' a story I heard about a ship called the *Lessing*. She ran ashore on the cliffs o' Clavers Geo, on Fair Isle, in thick fog on 23rd o' May, 1868. She was bound from Bremen to New York with 445 emigrants on board. Well, she plugged herself into the geo that tightly there was no room ta lower the boats and no one could expect to climb the slippery cliffs. On one side there was a peerie archway, only wide enough for a rowing boat, and as the passengers and crew were gathered on deck facing certain death, they saw the bow o' a Fair Isle yoal, manned by the men o' Fair Isle, come through the archway. There were several more and in a short space o' time every man, woman and child was ferried to the safety of Fair Isle."

"They were lucky," said another man, "those on the Dutch east Indiaman *Lastdrager* werna so fortunate when, in 1653, she was wrecked on the rocks o' Crussaness at Cullivoe. My goodness! They had had a terrible voyage, havin' been sent oot fae Holland, bound for Batavia in the Dutch East Indies. It was durin' the first Dutch/English war an' the authorities decided ta send her up through the Orkney/Shetland channel ta avoid the English. She sailed in early February an' on board were the crew an' passengers, numberin' some 206 souls, but sadly only 26 were to survive.

The house at Ravensgeo from the back, c.1950s.

"They passed within sight o' Fair Isle, but were caught in a gale fae the south-east and driven north until they sighted the Faroe Islands. Then the ship was struck by a huge wave that carried away all her boats and left her watter-logged an' listin' badly. As if that wasna enough the wind changed to blow from the north-west an' fae then on her fate was well an' truly sealed.

"It must have been terrible for all those folk on board her as she drifted for days at the mercy o' the sea. Still, they managed to keep her afloat by continuous pumpin' and bailin'. Then, on the 2nd o' March, in a fierce snowstorm, she rammed bow first into the rocks o' Crussaness."

The speaker paused and looked around the company as if seeking out any disagreement before continuing, "They say the stern broke clean aff an' them that didna go wi' her scrambled on tae the bow whaur they stayed till the tide came in again, afore either jumpin' or bein' washed overboard when the sea claimed the rest o' the vessel. Man o' man! It must have been really horrible for the men in the watter wi' waves throwin' heavy ships' timbers about. Even the

26 who managed ta crawl oot upon the rocks were aa wounded an' hurt by the splintery wood, but at least they found shelter in a peerie smithy on top o' the cliffs an' were saved." He looked around the circle of faces then added, "Anyway, that's the way I heard it."

"Yea," said another, "but their troubles didna end there for when the snow stopped an' the weather cleared they found twa chests o' silver an' fell oot over it. You see, some wanted ta share it aa oot amongst themsel's, but others, led by a young clerk o' the Dutch East India Company, Jan Camphuijs, determined to return it to the company."

"That is true," said the first speaker, "but it was old Ninian Neven, the Laird o' Windhouse, that took the silver and hid it for them. Not only that, but he put them in touch wi' a captain who sold them his ship. He lived on the Mainland in Laxfirth, so it meant a journey down there for Jan and his friend, the 'Gunner', and after a peerie while they fetched the ship up an' loaded the silver an' sailed for home."

"That's what happened true enough," said the other, "but before that they had a big fight, for only nine men followed honest Jan, but they were a valiant lot and beat off the larger force. They were lucky ta get their ship an' their silver an' head for home when they did, for a greater trouble had come on the land in the form o' the Governor o' Orkney, James Keith.

"On hearin' that there was a rich shipwreck he came north ta Yell wi' sixty armed men ta plunder the place in search o' riches. After he'd raided the Cullivoe area he turned his attention on the laird and his house, attacking it an' woundin' both Neven an' his daughter, Bessie, in a hail o' musket fire.

"So, the poor laird found himself bein' held prisoner, his home looted, his family and servants assaulted, whilst Keith and his ruffians ransacked and violated the neighbourhood."

"Yes," said one of the visitors, "he was little better than a vile plundering pirate, and North Yell was left the poorer for his visit ... just a rogue."

"But what about the Dutchmen?" asked another, "was any more ever heard from them?"

"Yes, yes," someone else spoke up, "the way I heard it was that they arrived back in Amsterdam in April o' 1653, an' the next year Jan Camphuijs sailed again for Batavia, an' he served his company well, for in due course he became the Governor o' the Dutch East Indies."

"He did well," the gruff voice sounded faint in my ears, "but his company never even said thanks to Ninian Neven for all the help he'd given the castaways ... no wonder he became such an embittered land grabbing old ... "

I didn't hear his ending for the heat of the peat fire and the hiss of the Tilley had lulled me into slumber.

Chapter Eight

Daa's Radar

"You better get your skates on if you're wantin' ta come aff wi' us," Uncle John's head, which had appeared around the door to deliver that statement disappeared again, but his voice added, "we'll be leavin' in five minutes."

Hurriedly, I pulled on my socks and began to hunt for my footwear. I hoped they wouldn't go to the fishing without me and I knew I might be very unpopular if I caused them any delay.

This was the second week of our holidays and the chance of a day off fishing in the boat was not to be missed. Mum and Dad had returned to Virkie, leaving us to enjoy a few more weeks in our favourite place.

I pulled on my shoes and went through to the but end, not expecting many of the family to still be there, but I was wrong. Daa, Uncle John, Hamish, Rose and Aunt Bertha were seated at the table finishing their breakfast. Granny was by the fire stirring the remaining gruel so that it wasn't stuck to the pot by the time I came through.

It was an open fire with the pot hung on a 'crook' above the burning peats. The crook chain was attached to the crook 'bauk', a beam fixed across the chimney above the fire. On each side of the fireplace was an armchair and along the back wall was a large press upon which stood the fine Tilley lamp that lit the hours of darkness.

When you entered the room the first smells you noticed were paraffin, peat-smoke and salt fish. The fish were hanging on 'raeps' (lines of rope or strong string fixed along the ceiling). In these so-called enlightened days most people would be horrified to have such powerful scents in their ultra-modern homesteads, but in the far-off days of my childhood nearly all croft houses had their raeps of fish in the roof, and were fuelled by peats and paraffin. Perhaps people were not so hygienically orientated, but I doubt if we were any the worse for that. After all, our immune systems were probably far better than those of the super clean kids of today.

Shyly, I went up to the table, as Uncle John glanced at me and asked, "Runnin' late this mornin', Jock?"

I gave an embarrassed smile, and sitting down began to tuck into the food Granny set in front of me.

"A right Hungry Horace," Hamish said with a grin, "isn't he?"

I didn't really mind their teasing. Uncle John was the only one to call me 'Jock', but 'Horace' was given to me just because I liked my food. Many years later I was to meet old school friends from southern Shetland who still knew me by that name even though I was never fat and did not encourage its use.

Suddenly Bertha addressed me, saying, "Are you comin' wi' me this morning, John Arnold?"

"Eh? What?" I was suddenly filled with a dread that she would claim my company and I would miss the fishing trip.

"Well," she explained, "I have to go to Linkshouse shop, and then to the Co-op at Hillend, and after that I thought we'd go to visit Andrew and Teenie ... I would think you might'a' liked that."

I failed to realise that she was teasing me, and hardly daring to breathe in case they sided with her, I replied, "I'm goin' fishin' wi' Daa an' Uncle John."

"Oh, fishin'," she said with a sniff, "man, I would think you'd have enjoyed shoppin' far more."

"Na, I dunna think so."

"Well," pretending offence she sniffed loudly and continued, "if you don't want to come I'll just have to tak' Rose." She smiled down at Rose who nodded without much enthusiasm. Perhaps she had also had other plans for the day.

"That's fine." Bertha's eyes, travelling to her father, brother and Hamish, had a definite twinkle in them, so I realised she'd only been joking. Looking again at Rose she said, "We'll maybe tak' Mary wi' us too."

"Well," Daa said suddenly, putting down his tea cup, "anybody going fishin' wi' me had better eat up for I'm finished." Then glancing at his son he asked, "Are you ready?"

"Yea," John replied, "just about."

Then to me, "Come on Jock, eat up."

My spoon moved at high speed as the gruel was shovelled into my mouth. Rising from the table Uncle John grinned at Hamish as they both turned to watch me.

"You're right," he said, "Hungry Horace in the comic has nothin' on him."

By the time I'd finished eating and put my rubber boots on the fishing party had gone. As I left the house I saw Aunt Annie and Aunt Mary talking to two women of the neighbourhood, Lizzie Pole and Annie o' Houl. Before they could see me I dodged around the porch and out of their sight, then hared out the far gate and down the green to put the lambie house between us ... nothing was going to stop me going off in the boat.

John Arnold, Daa and Hamish in Mid Yell.

When I arrived at the boat noost Hamish and John were laying down the linns (pieces of wood over which the boat would be pulled, making the task so much easier). All the gear was already aboard, so in no time at all the boat was on her way to the sea and soon I was seated in the stern, dangling my fingers in the water trying to catch the lucky-lines, as Daa rowed the boat off from the shore. Lucky-lines are long strands of stringy seaweed, perhaps so called after the Norse trickster god, Loki.

Hamish was up in the bows watching all that was going on with eager eyes. Uncle John took an oar from Daa and sat down to row. They seemed content to do the rowing themselves but often they would let us row out to the fishing grounds.

In the moment when the rowing stopped during the change over, when John took an oar from Daa, my hand closed over a length of seaweed strands and I pulled strongly. The trouble with sitting in the stern was that everything you did was seen by whoever was rowing. My action earned me a disapproving stare from Daa and a growled, "Tak' your hands oot o' the watter boy, an' behave yoursel'."

I did as bid and sat staring at my feet for a few moments, but it was such a lovely day that I just had to look about me again. The distant hills seemed to have a few fingers of mist cloaking their tops and although the sun was shining the hills seemed to be greying down.

The men had also noticed this and Daa said to John, "Day's changin', might be misty later."

"Yeah," was the reply, "but it might keep clear 'til dark."

"Hmmm," Daa sounded doubtful.

I was always just as interested in what was happening along the shoreline than I was in what was going on in the boat and once we almost put ashore again when I suddenly called out, "Oh! Look. There's a cat among the ebb-stones!"

Daa, and to a lesser extent Uncle John, were, like many other fishermen of the time, inclined to be superstitious about the sea and fishing, and to mention a cat by its proper name was almost too much to be borne. It would have been alright had I used one of the seaman's names for it, like the skaaven (shaver) or the voaler (wailer), but to call a cat a cat was really asking for bad luck. I was left in no doubt that if we caught no fish the blame would be laid at my door and if that happened it would be unlikely that I would ever be taken off fishing again.

Superstitious grown-ups meant that there were many dos and don'ts about boats and fishing, for instance, when pushing the boat off from the beach she had to be turned sungaets (with the sun, clockwise), never widdergaets (anti-clockwise).

You had to watch what you said for offending the sea-spirits and bringing bad luck. We learned over the years many of the substitute words to use for things seen on land, like boorik for a cow, russie for a horse or pony, cunnie for a rabbit and bonbiter for a dog. Even parts of the boat had their special names and we children soon picked these things up, but we also realised that we could do a little teasing by not using the nicknames.

So, as the boat was rowed towards the mouth of Mid Yell Voe, I became aware that Hamish was softly whistling a tune to himself, but I couldn't just hear what it was. Suddenly, Daa glanced over his shoulder at him and asked, "Boy, are you whistlin' up a wind? Give yon lark up."

The whistling stopped and a slight smile crossed Hamish's face. He saw me looking at him and grinned. I'd also caught the glimmer of a smile on Uncle John's face and realised that perhaps he was not quite as superstitious as I'd thought him to be.

I waited until we were approaching the Head of Hevdagarth before I called to Hamish, "Look, there's a rabbit, Hamish." It was true, we often saw rabbits around there, but it earned me cold frowning stares from the men on the oars.

Then Hamish pointed shoreward and cried, "There's another rabbit, John, doon apon yon green bit near the banks."

"Yes," I agreed, "there's a lot o' rabbits there the day."

"Wheest wi' dee boy!" Daa had had enough naming of the unnameable. "We'll catch naethin' the day wi' you sayin' things lik' yon."

Soon, however, we were out of the voe and set to fishing, with Daa, Uncle John and Hamish fishing and myself on the oars. Soon

Daa began hauling in his line again with a look of joy on his face. He always became excited when fish took the hooks and he usually had a good idea what kind of fish he'd caught just by the feel of the line.

"Boys-a-boys!" he cried, "hit's mackerel boys, an' they're havin' a right dance too. One on every hook I'd say." Then, to the fish, "Oh! Come to me my peerie darlins!"

A pause whilst he looked deep into the water, straining to see the first flashes of light as the fish became visible, when he would shout, "There's a light in the lioom, boys!"

By now Uncle John and Hamish were hauling in too, excitement on their faces.

"Aye," John cried, "an' they're welcome to come."

"Yes," Hamish agreed, hauling in desperately, "but they're makin' a good fight o' it."

Mackerel are a lively fish and soon there were a few dozen wriggling and flapping in the bottom of the boat. The hand-lines were soon cast again and for a moment I watched Hamish's arm rise and fall as he worked the line over the stern. John and Daa were likewise working and waiting for fish to bite. Then Daa began to haul in his line and I eagerly asked, "Have you caught somethin', Daa?"

He shook his head saying, "Wait till John an' Hamish have pulled in their lines a bit an' then row on slowly. Mind, don't be too hasty or they'll catch bottom an' you'll be in trouble."

I did as he asked and rowed slowly on until we were lying between Baa Taing on the island of Hascosay and the Ness of Vatsetter on Yell. Then the fish began coming aboard again, haddock, whiting and then mackerel again. The latter so numerous now, there was a good chance of tangled lines.

It was when hoes (dogfish) became involved that Daa called a halt.

"There's a fog comin' down so we'd best mak' for the noost."

John, unhooking a hoe and throwing it back into the water said, "Yea, an' a right steekit stumba too, by the looks o' it. Anyway, the hoes are ruinin' our fishin' ... see you dis," he held up a mackerel which had a large bite wound on its back, "they're eatin' them apon the hook."

It was only when Daa mentioned it that I realised the mist was creeping closer now. Like a grey army it came pressing closer from all sides as if trying to trap us in the centre.

Looking east I could see nothing of the island of Fetlar, and to the north only the shoreline of Hascosay was visible. To the south and west all was hidden by a bank of thick fog. Uncle John was the first to get his hand-line wound up, saying, "Get yourself back in the stern, Jock, I'll tak' the oars. Mind, sit in peace."

Swiftly I clambered back into my seat in the stern as he took over the oars. By the time we'd done that the fog had overtaken us and I could hardly see Hamish in the bow.

"Row for the voe," Daa said, as he finished winding up his hand-line. "We'll just have ta tak' it as it comes."

As John began to row the blades of the oars seemed to dip into a haziness that appeared to be more mist than water. After a little, Daa said, "Aandoo boy," (this meant to stop the boat's forward motion and keep her steady in one place by gently rowing against the tide), "an' dan stop a moment till I see what's what."

John did as he was bid and stopped the boat, then aandooed for a little before leaning on the oars, listening, aandooing very gently to keep our position.

Daa slowly stood up and held a hand to his ear, whilst I, wondering what he was doing, opened my mouth to ask, and enquire how were we to find our way home, but I caught Uncle John's eye and the look in his said, "Wheest noo." So the question was never asked.

Daa stood listening for a minute or two. Then, with a glance at John explained, "We're past the Ness o' Vatsetter, an' we've gone nearly up to Hascosay Sound for I hear the watter on the point o' the Gunnald. Row you a peerie bit more ta port dis time." So sayin, he sat down and John began rowing briskly again, but I couldn't tell if he was rowing to port or not.

Soon we stopped again and Daa stood up listening, but to young, inexperienced ears like mine the sounds about the boat were loud enough to cover the more distant ones. Water lapped both outside and in, dying fish made slapping noises as they vainly fought their destiny on the tilfers (the loose floor planking on the bottom of

Andrew Leask (Daa) and Hamish in the old black boat.

the boat). There was the sound of the boat herself, creaking and groaning as she rose and fell with the swell. Then, somewhere nearby a bird called hauntingly in the mist, and closer, almost alongside, a family of neesiks (porpoises) broke surface with a sudden blow of air.

"Yea," Daa said, "we're not far from the Ness noo. Row you on a bit."

I knew it was not the Ness, or Headland of Vatsetter he was referring to now, but the Ness of Lüssetter, so we were a little nearer home.

Daa remained standing as John rowed on, until even I was able to hear the waves on the rocks and was beginning to worry lest we ran onto them. Daa, however, was in no doubt as to where we were and presently he sat down and took the oars.

I began to help Uncle John and Hamish gut the fish, throwing the unwanted bits over the side. Even with thick fog this action was seen by sharp-eyed gulls and seconds after the first lot was thrown we were being mobbed by hungry birds. The fact that I had not caught any of the fish bothered me not in the least, even without any fish I'd have enjoyed the day out in the boat.

Almost before I realised it the boat was grounding on the beach at the noost below the house … and just as quickly the fog was thinning out and soon the sun would be shining out again.

Presently, with the fish ashore, any water bailed out of the boat, and her once more pulled up into her place in the noost, Daa began stringing some of the fish together until he had several strung-up bunches of fine fish. I watched warily knowing that with Hamish, and Rose who had now joined us, I would be sent with fish to the neighbouring houses, whilst John and Daa dealt with those left. Some would be eaten right away but the bulk of our catch would be salted and eaten during the winter.

Being a shy little boy I hated having to go visiting people's houses, even when the inhabitants were closely related, but with Hamish and Rose with me perhaps it wouldn't be too bad.

The first house we visited was that belonging to the parents of our friends, Billy and Basil, which cheered me somewhat. After the fish had been handed over and we made our excuses, saying that we had to get home again for our dinner, Billy and Basil came outside with us but were warned not to go far as their food was almost on the table.

"Have you got the tent up wi' you?" Billy asked.

"Yes," Hamish replied, "we'll go out this weekend."

"Fine." Both boys were as eager for a camping trip as we were.

"What about the morn?" Hamish asked, "I thought we could go tae the piltocks." As if he hadn't just come ashore from a fishing trip he was eager to go on another. However, I knew that this time he meant to fish from the old pier below the shop at Ravensgeo where there were always plenty sillocks and piltocks. These fish are better known outside Shetland as coalfish, but in the islands they have numerous names. In the first year it is sillock, becoming a piltock in its second year. It spends at least four years close inshore but then swims out into deeper water where it spends its life as an adult saed (saithe).

So it was settled that the two boys would come down the next morning and, if our grown-ups had nothing else planned for us to do, we would get our gear and go fishing.

There were at least two strings yet to deliver, and as soon as we returned to the house Rose was called inside, Hamish sent in one direction and I in the other. My route was now up through Burrapark to Gardie and I'd been given orders to fetch the milk down as I was going to that croft ... most decidedly I was not amused.

Yet once I'd been there, fussed over and was on my way home again, my mood improved. Davy Anderson's pony was in the park and after shaking its head and rolling an eye at me it proceeded to follow me down over the braes. I paused beside the pond once I was over the fence, and turning, made a face at the animal. It had been a bit un-nerving to have it dogging my footsteps, especially as I hadn't had much dealings with ponies since I was six or seven. However, horses and ponies have always been some of my favourite animals and I enjoyed the experience.

At last I left the pond and hurried down to the house where I was swiftly ordered to come inside and get out of my rubber boots.

What delight it was to sit down to a feast of fish livers, oatmeal and potatoes. The others might also enjoy the fish, but for me those three items were like the ambrosia of the Olympian gods and I ate until I could eat no more.

Chapter Nine

In the Whelk Ebb

Next morning I was up and out of bed much earlier, excited about going to the piltocks with Hamish and the Guthrie boys. However, it was not to be. As soon as breakfast was over I was sent to the well to get water.

Carrying the two water buckets I set out. The path to the well was across the road and along the back of the shop. As I went I could see Daa up in the top of the small field cutting hay with a sye (scythe), but he was facing away from me so did not acknowledge my presence.

Sometimes people used to put eels, or a tiny trout, into their wells in the belief that the fish would keep the water fresh and clean. As I raised the wooden lid I gazed down into the water to see if there was any sign of the fish reputed to be there, but saw nothing but a few bubbles and a pebble or two on the bottom.

With some care I lowered the enamelled buckets into the well one at a time. Once full they were quite heavy for an eleven-year-old boy and it was all I could do to carry them a few steps without sloshing water all over my legs and into the rubber boots I'd put on.

Daa was busy sharpening his sye, but paused long enough to laugh and call down to me, "You're gettin' your legs washed now, John Arnold."

"I'm no' spillin' a drop," I shouted back.

I was repaid for that untruth by the water splashing even higher and as I exclaimed "Uugh!" at its sudden coldness, Daa laughed and called, "Oh, yes. I can see that."

Surprisingly, by the time I returned to the porch where the buckets were kept they were still almost three-quarters full.

"Oh, John Arnold, you've done well," said one of my aunts, "so as a reward you can go up to Brown's shop for some messages for

Daa makes hay at Ravensgeo.

us. I've got a list. You'll maybe get a sweetie too, for going."

Inwardly I groaned. This day was not turning out to be anything like I'd planned.

"Whaur's Hamish?" I cried, "he's older than me so he should go, an' I got in the watter."

"I wish I knew whaur he's gone," she said, "I had lots o' things I wanted him to do, but he's sneaked away. Likely he's gone up to see Billy, or one of his pals. Just wait till he comes back, I'll have a few words to say to him."

I felt that I'd like to say something to him myself, but there was nothing I could do about it now. I tried another tack, "Whaur's Rose?"

"Oh, she's away somewhere wi' Mary."

There was to be no escape and I began to wish I'd sneaked away myself as with the list in one hand and shopping bag in the other I went out the door.

As I was passing Daa on my way up the road he grinned and asked, "Goin' shoppin'?"

"It's no fair," I said, "Hamish shoulda been here ta help me."

"Never you mind," he smiled, "there'll maybe be somethin' more interestin' for you ta do when you come back."

That did nothing to cheer me up as 'something more interesting' very likely meant more work, when what I really desired was more play, or at least work of my own choosing.

I was lucky at the shop as there were no other customers. It was as Mrs Brown dealt with my order and I saw her reach for a piece of salt skate that I recalled the story about Daa and the skate.

Times were still pretty hard in the years just after the war ended and folk were glad to get any kind of food they could. Fish

The ruins of Heather Cottage.

were plentiful, but a change from the usual kinds – haddock, whiting, piltock and mackerel – was very welcome. One day a large skate was seen swimming on the surface. Sometimes skate had trouble with enlarged livers and once they became too big the fish could not dive. The skate in question had obviously made its way into Mid Yell Voe and was now swimming on a course that would take it by Daa's noost and up into the head of the voe.

Daa knew that if he let the fish go by his noost he would very likely lose it to someone else. His boat, however, was pulled up in the noost and there seemed to be no chance of him getting his hand on it. A lesser man might have given up there ... but not Daa.

Throwing off his jacket, jumper and boots, he ran down to the beach and dived into the water. He might have been a stout man but he was also powerfully strong and a fine swimmer ... that skate had no chance. Presently he emerged from the sea with the water running from his moustaches, a delightful gleam in his eye and the skate in his arms.

I left the shop much happier than I'd entered for, having seen me standing there with a large smile on my face, the good lady said it was fine to see a boy who enjoyed shopping and gave me a sweetie.

I went over the fence into Burrapark, which was a shortcut we often used. As I went down the field I hardly noticed that the shopping bag was heavy for my mind was still on Daa. I paused to stand for a moment looking at the road up to the shop remembering how, to win a bet, Daa had one day carried a 'bowe' bag of flour, weighing 140 lbs, from the pier at Ravensgeo up to Brown's shop. This came about because he worked on the 'flit' boat that brought flour and other goods to the bakeries at Gardiestaing and Ravensgeo, and both shops. The steamer *Earl of Zetland* came into Mid Yell Voe, but could not dock at Linkshouse pier, so the 'flit' boats transferred the goods ashore.

From the landing-place at Ravensgeo to Brown's shop was a good distance and uphill most of the way, but Daa didn't let go the bag until he arrived at the shop. After that demonstration of strength we boys often gave Daa the nickname of 'Old Bowe'.

I was almost at the bottom fence when, looking towards

Gardie, I saw Hamish with pals, Jim, Billy and Basil, leaving the Gerts (Garths), the Guthrie boys' home. The four boys did not appear to be heading toward Ravensgeo, but were walking up through Gardie.

I wanted to shout for them to wait for me and as soon as I put the shopping to the house I'd join them, but just as I opened my mouth to shout they disappeared behind a house, so I just growled inwardly and continued on my way.

I saw no sign of my grandfather as I came back onto the road again and hurried down to the house. However, on entering the building I found that he had stopped for a cup of tea. Uncle John was also there and as I came in he was saying, "I'm telling you, there's so many folk around here that like to spread a good story I reckon I could start a tale in the morning and it would come back to me later on wi' so many additions I would hardly recognise it."

"But John," said Aunt Annie, "not everybody is like that."

"Maybe not," he grinned, "but if you choose the right person to begin wi' they'd soon set it on its way."

"Na, na," said Granny Katie, "it surely wouldn't come back that quick ... maybe in a week or two." Not seeing the teasing twinkle in her eye John shrugged and said some day he would prove his point.

For a moment granny and the aunts fussed over me, telling me what a good job I'd done, and in no time at all I was sitting at the table with a cup of sweet, milky tea in my hand and the crumbs from a large biscuit sparkling on the front of my jumper.

"Well, Jock," asked Uncle John, "are you coming whelkin' wi' me today?"

I nearly spilt my tea. "Eh?" I asked beaming a smile, "whaur are we goin'?"

"Whalfirth." He gave me a mock scowl, "So you'd better be ready an' fit for a good long walk an' some mighty hard work."

I declared I was ready and would manage to walk with ease.

We left Ravensgeo and climbed up the braes to the Gerts, but there was no sign of any boys about the place. Usually we would have visited all the houses on our way, but this day Uncle John obviously didn't want to be delayed as he'd planned it so the tide would be well and truly on its way out when we reached the beach at Whalfirth Voe.

When we arrived at the Gardie road we walked along until we came to its end at the old quarry above Gardie Ness, the last house. Then we crossed the fence and walked up over the braes until we came to the little house in which I'd been born.

"Well, John Arnold," my uncle asked with a grin, "d'you remember livin' here?"

"Yes." The house was fast becoming a ruin and I felt sorry for that as I had many fond memories of the happy times we spent there, "I always liked Heather Cottage."

We had lived there during the war years, but if I had happy wartime memories, Uncle John did not, and recalling how badly he'd been wounded I said no more, but idly kicked at a stone and followed him along the front of the house and out beyond the dilapidated outbuildings to the fence. A stenkle (wheatear) flew from a post out onto a stone on the hillside. Whenever you walked in the hills stenkles were chattering and scolding you for invading their territory.

From here we could see the big house of Windhouse in its picturesque setting on a hill overlooking the road to West Yell. I knew its story pretty well having listened to the grown-ups telling stories on dark winter's evenings.

There had been a house there from the 1400s, but the house had been about a hundred yards further up the hill. In 1707 they moved the whole house down to its present site, stone by stone. Then in 1880 it was reconstructed to become the house we see today: a one and a half storey villa. It has castellated side wings, crowsteps and, above the door, an armorial panel of its original owners, the Neven family.

It was, and is, an imposing sight and the fact that it is said to be the most haunted house in the islands does not help when you are eleven and know that your path lies by its door.

Windhouse is on the east side of Whalfirth Voe, and part of my mind wanted to visit the building whilst the rest of it worried about ghosts.

There was said to be a lady in silk who rustled around in one of the rooms; a tall man in a long black cloak who rises up out of the ground outside the kitchen window and walks through the wall; then there was said to be the sound of a crying child. Once, during some alterations, a baby's skeleton was found in the kitchen wall, and that of a woman found buried at the foot of the stairs. Perhaps the most frightening was the story of a large black dog said to prowl around the bedrooms. There was also the tale of the trow, or troll, that came every year to attack the house on Christmas Eve, until one year a sea captain, armed with an axe, chased the trow back to Mid Yell Voe and killed him almost on the seashore at the head of the voe.

The grave of the trow just happened to be only feet away from one of our grandfather's peat banks, so we were used to that story.

As we left Gardie and walked down over the heathery braes of the area known as 'The Back of the Ness', I knew Uncle John was checking the sheep as he went, almost automatically counting any of Daa's we came across, and taking note of their health and well-being. Even I could see this year's lambs were growing well.

It didn't take us long to get down to where Laxa Burn meets the sea. I would have gone down on the beach once we passed the krö (sheepfold), but John headed along for the bridge over the burn so I followed. We made better time once we were on the road. No tarmacadam in those days, but mortar roads that could have your eyes filled with particles of gritty dust if there was any wind.

This day, however, was calm and it was a pleasure to walk along. We didn't go in silence, nor in chatter, but with occasional bursts of talk.

"Are we going to Windhouse?" I asked.

"Maybe pop along," he answered, "see if there's any ghosts around."

"Have you ever seen one there?"

"Oh, hundreds," he joked as he watched me, as if expecting me to show fear. Then, "No, John Arnold, I've never seen one. Ach, there were said to be bad things that happened there, an' maybe bad folk lived there, but I doubt if any have come back to haunt folk."

"You don't believe in ghosts?"

"Doesna matter what I believe, you mak' up your own mind.

An' remember, a ghost is just somebody that's died. Yis, an' if they didna try to harm folk when they were livin', they're hardly likely to do harm when they are dead."

I had never thought about it like that before and I figured he might have a point. I was quiet, thinking about it as we walked on towards the brig over the Burn of Setter.

Setter lies across from Windhouse on the south side of the road, seeming to nestle there at the foot of the Hill of Setter.

At last we came to Windhouse lodge and turned right to follow the road that ran a little way up the hill. We did not go right up to the croft house at the road's end, but branched off to follow the now overgrown way up to the haunted house.

Windhouse had been empty for years, but there was someone working at something just outside the building at the back and Uncle John went over to lean on the wall and speak to him. I followed, a little sorry that my uncle had not gone in by the front gate, but had cut up over the braes just outside the wall ... I would have liked to have gone into the house.

As I waited I spent the time just looking at the house and I did not feel as if a ghost would jump out at me. In fact, I felt it to be a rather peaceful place.

From Windhouse we went down over the hillside to the east shore of Whalfirth Voe and began to work along the beach gathering whelks, which would be sold once Uncle John collected enough to make it worthwhile. The whelks would live well enough in sacks left on the beach in the water, or where they could be covered by the incoming tide, until he was ready to send them to the buyer.

It was a job that required a lot of bending and it didn't take long for muscles to start protesting, but we kept on searching for whelks amongst the seaweed and rocks along the shore. It was a warm day too and we were soon over-heating with the unusual exertions.

We stopped for a break and Uncle John produced some sandwiches and a biscuit or two and we sat on the largest of the rocks to enjoy our simple repast.

Then, back to work again, and here I might say that my uncle seemed to be far and away the best at the job, finding them faster than I could ever hope to though I did try my best to keep up.

At last the tide turned and the sea began to creep back up the beach and soon where we were working would be under water.

"Ach," said John, mopping his brow, "this is an awful way to mak' a living, eh Jock?" Then he grinned, saying, "Come on, let's get this sack tied up an' then we'll head for home. We've no' done bad for one day."

By the time we arrived back at the house we were tired and hungry and pleased to see that the women were preparing food.

Hamish was in a very black mood as he and his pals had come on several youths playing football using a hedgehog as a ball. Hamish was as much an animal lover as myself, and this act of cruelty had infuriated him, but sadly his intervention came too late for the poor animal.

We often found hedgehogs around Ravensgeo and knowing what great wanderers they are we once tried an experiment. Whenever we found one we would put a tiny spot of white paint on its back and release it. This was to tell us how far it had travelled when it was next discovered. Only later did I realise that other people seeing these hedgehogs must have wondered why each one had a spot of white on their prickly backs ... perhaps a new variation?

On the other hand, some of them might well have lost their spots quickly, which could be why there was no great rush by the animal-attuned to see the Spotted Hedgehogs of Mid Yell.

Hamish declared that in the morning he was going to put up his tent and that weekend we'd camp out. We would have liked to have gone away somewhere up into the hills, but knew that in that case Daa would not have let us go alone, so we would not camp so far away from the house. There were other lads coming too – Billy, Basil and our old friend, John Williamson, who was at that time staying across the water in North-a-Voe.

That evening turned damp with occasional showers of drizzly rain so we stayed in and had an evening of games. When the weather was bad we often spent the time playing card games and numerous board games. Old Daa loved a game of draughts and would ponder over the men on the board before making his, often winning, moves.

Another game loved by us all was the card game, euchre. Sometimes as a game progressed Uncle John would accuse his father of cheating, whereupon Daa would deny this with furiously waggling moustaches and the game would continue with light-hearted banter between the two. Looking back on it now, I'm not sure that this wasn't a double-act to put other players off their guard, but one thing I'm sure of is that we all enjoyed ourselves ... perhaps Daa more than anyone else.

We also liked Monopoly, but not being able to afford to buy a new game Hamish made one and we, and our friends, often played that on wet days and evenings.

In summer, when it didn't get dark until after midnight, we spent fine evenings playing outside until ordered into the house by grown-ups. We spent a good deal of time on the beach, or up at the pond behind the house, where we would sail boats made from old dried-milk tins, opened out and bent into the shape of a boat. Some would have a sail and nearly all had a tiny seat in the centre which helped to keep the shape. Invariably they sank in any but the calmest sailing conditions, but at least the pond was no depth so they were easily retrieved. Not so if we sailed them in the sea when they were likely to be gone forever.

We also enjoyed flying kites, but unlike the fine plastic kites of today, we had to make our own out of thin sticks, brown paper and lots of thread and string ... but oh, the wonderful feeling of delight when the craft you had formed with your own hands took flight and soared high into the sky.

In play we often used long dock stems as spears and decorated our wooden swords with silver or coloured paper, usually from sweetie wrappers.

Once, Hamish decided to make a really special bow and arrows. The arrows were easily whittled from wood, but the bow was a different matter until he found the handle of a metal bucket. The bucket itself had long since been discarded, but the handle was strong enough to make a powerful bow, providing he could find the right bowstring. For a while he pondered this problem until he found an old car tyre with the inner tube still inside. It did not take him long to cut a length of rubber from the tube.

That day it wasn't only us children who were at the trial of the new bow. Daa and Uncle John were there too, eager to have a shot. Then, when they realised how powerful it was, we were warned not to shoot at each other with it. I suppose they had mental pictures of one of the cowboys being riddled with fast-flying arrows.

Hamish had a quick and inventive mind and was often to be found writing poetry about the people he knew; or busily planning some interesting expedition usually connected with the sea, boats or fish. Now the most important thing on his mind was the forthcoming camping trip and, even if we were not going far, this trip would be one of the highlights of our holidays and we were determined to have a really interesting time.

Chapter Ten

War and Peace

I was awakened next morning by the putt-putt sound of the bakery engine as it was started for another day's work. Hamish was already up and spooning gruel into his mouth when I came through.

"Are we goin' to put the tent up?" I asked eagerly.

He nodded his head, saying, "Yes, it's a fine day for it."

It is difficult to rush through breakfast when you have three aunts and a grandmother trying to make sure you eat properly and at a sensible, if slow, speed.

Presently, however, we set off with the tent to a flat grassy area just beyond Anderson Station. This had, at one time, been a herring station and is where the fish factory stands today.

We sited the tent where we thought it would be fairly dry and protected on the south side by the braes below the Gerts. We would need no shelter that day for the weather was fine and set to remain so for the next few days.

We were soon joined by our pals and there was much fun and lots of good natured banter as we struggled to get the tent up. Hamish was in charge so it would be put up correctly and he would not be satisfied until it was all ship-shape and Bristol fashion.

At last, though, he was able to stand back, cast his eyes over the tent, and say, "It's fine, boys, but it's a pity there's nothin' ta cover the ground inside wi' ... the grass is that wet." There were no waterproof ground sheets for us, only the hope that the grass would dry up by bedtime.

After a while we left the tent and wandered back toward the house. As we went we played a wild game of cowboys and Indians, a favourite game at the time. The only problem was that Hamish, Billy and our other friends were older, and claimed the right to be cowboys. Basil and I ended up whooping and hollerin' and waving our dock spears as we Indians charged, only to be shot down by imaginary Colt 45s or Springfield rifles, and told to lie down as we'd been shot long ago.

We didn't like always being Indians and would long to play the cowboys, but our complaints went unheeded and we would end up in severe sulkulation. At that time Indians were still looked on as being the baddies and the cowboys the heroes. Only later on, when we were far too old to play imaginary games, would we realise that there was as much good in the red man as there was in the white, and that the native American people were rightfully trying to protect their lands from the rapacious white settlers.

Sometimes we would play cops and robbers and as often as not we younger boys ended up as the robbers ... there seemed to be no justice for us.

Then there were times when the sheriff and his deputy would hunt down the outlaws. We tried to give them a good run for their money, but really we had no hope against the two-gun sheriff and his ferocious deputy. Rose too, would join in our games sometimes, and whilst she might have been the youngest, and a girl, she had a mind of her own and no sheriff, cowboy or cop was going to tell her what to do. If she had to be an Indian then some cowboy was about to be scalped.

It was all great fun, but I think she enjoyed the rough and tumble games as much as those played with other girls, and dolls. On this day, however, Rose was away doing something else and we were too intent on camping to play many other games. It wasn't long before we returned to the campsite and by then we had been joined by one or two other pals and were set on having a splendid time.

I am not sure now what actually began the trouble, but when it came it was serious enough to cause a breach in our friendship that ended in a severe case of fisticuffs. We had fallen out before, but not quite as badly as this.

Now it seemed that it was us brothers against the rest, and it began with each side shouting insults; violent, aggressive, strong-worded insults where the older boys were concerned.

No doubt we could be heard a good distance away and old Daa, working about his boat at the noost below the house, certainly heard the uproar and realised that before long noses would be bleeding and eyes blackened. He set off at the run to get there and stop the fight before damage was done but before he was a quarter of the way to us we had charged the others. Soon, Hamish and Billy were involved in a furious half wrestling, half boxing match, which ended with them rolling on the ground.

Basil tried to stop me by an attempted trip-up as I chased one of the other lads. The boy had been shouting insults as loudly as any and I was determined to give him a good hiding. He ran for the steep braes behind the campsite and was halfway up when my hand fastened on his ankle. He kicked at me wildly with his free foot but I held on, sure that instead of climbing up the brae he was coming back down to get the trouncing I thought he deserved.

"John Arnold, let that boy's leg go." That was Daa and he sounded all riled up. Glancing in the direction of his voice I saw him standing there with a hand on Hamish's shoulder.

Billy was now halfway up the braes with the other boys, but he paused to shout back at Hamish, "You couldna fight your way oot o' a henhoose."

I saw Hamish start forward in anger but Daa clamped a hand on his shoulder and said something in his ear that calmed Hamish down again.

The other boy wriggled free from my grasp and I made an instinctive grab for him but Daa had seen the move.

"John Arnold. Come down here at once."

I went, looking mutinous and scowling.

"A fine pair your are," Daa said, "fightin' wi' your pals lik' that. Well, there'll be no campin' for you this night. Aye, an' maybe not even this weekend. That will depend on how you behave from now on."

"Oh, Daa ... " Hamish began, only to be quelled by a look.

"Now," ordered our irate grandfather, "back to the house. Why, you're not fit to be allowed out on your own."

As we approached the house we discovered that it was not

only Daa who had heard the commotion, for outside the porch were several figures watching our progress.

"A right pair o' fightin' Strachans we've got here," said Daa as we were marched up to the porch, "just brawlin' over at Anderson Station."

There were several exclamations of disapproval and shocked clucking sounds, and one of our aunts tutted and said, "Well, you know, it's in the blood."

We knew what she meant by that. Our father and his six brothers had earned a reputation as fighters in their young days. We also knew that there was a difference between them and us as much of their fighting had been done in friendly bouts, or competitive matches, just to prove they were better than the men who took them on. We had fought in anger and with the intention of hurting our opponents and that would not be tolerated.

We were in disgrace, confined to the house, with the threat of some kind of punishment hanging over our heads, which was made all the harder to bear as we knew that outside the sun was shining and our tent was waiting, empty and unattended.

That evening Daa decided that, possibly, the other boys were just as much to blame as we were, so the only punishment we would undergo would be a one night ban on camping. However, we would go with him up to the Gerts to make friends again with Billy and Basil.

This duly happened and there were several shamefaced boys in the Gerts that night as their parents and our grandfather made sure that we knew how near we'd come to landing in serious trouble and would certainly be severely punished should we disgrace ourselves in like manner again.

Later, when we'd at last escaped from our elders, Hamish turned to Billy and asked, "Are you goin' to tak' back what you said about me an' a henhouse?"

Billy removed his glasses and, cleaning them on his hanky said, "I just said it 'cause I was angry. I didna really mean it."

"Okay," Hamish grinned, "anyway, we'd better be good peerie boys from now on or Old Bowe will sort us out."

Of course, boys being boys there were many more

disagreements, arguments and falling-outs, but never again were we to come so near to hurting one another.

When we returned home it was to find Uncle John in a cheerful mood as he had proved that he was right about the speed gossip travelled around the island. That morning he had told someone that two very unlikely islanders were courting, and in the afternoon the story had come back to him greatly exaggerated.

"Is yon no' awful?" Granny Katie said, "tellin' lies about poor harmless old folk lik' them." Then to Uncle John, "You should be ashamed o' yoursel'."

"It was an experiment," he retorted, "an' when folk see that there's nothing going on between them they'll realise that it was just a story and did no harm."

"Well," Granny said sternly, "just mind what happened when somebody told a story about Old Tirval o' the Wast Neeps and Osla o' Skrottirigs."

We had all heard that story and it went as follows:

One day some bright spark had told Old Rasmie of Luggahill that Tirval was known to be courting Osla from Skrottirigs croft. Soon a full-blown story was going around which said that they were now engaged and the wedding date was set. Old Osla was going to sell Skrottirigs and live happily ever after out along the Wast Neeps.

This story was so convincing that after a few days people got to believing it to be a fact, so that when the two old people came, at different times, to the shop, they were bombarded with questions about their forthcoming marriage. Highly embarrassed and furiously angry they each attempted to nip such wicked rumours in the bud.

Things might have quietened down after that given time and no more questions, but destiny does not often go by the easiest way and fate set Old Rasmie of Luggahill and an enraged Tirval on converging paths. Upon their meeting Rasmie made some sly comments about courting couples and expressed a desire to be invited to the wedding. Tirval was now so angry that he raised his stick and threatened to brain Old Rasmie if he uttered another word. Rasmie backed away from the irate crofter who followed him for a few yards, poking him and shaking his stick to accompany each word, as he snarled, "There-is-no-romance. No-courtship. I-cannot-abide-the-old-witch. Therefore-there-is-no-marriage. Be-gone-from-my-sight-you-wicked-old-reprobate."

Rasmie, old as he was, was not a fellow to be pushed and prodded by anyone's walking stick and swiftly declared that if a certain old goat prodded him once more he would break the stick over the fellow's head.

At that point someone stepped in to stop any more trouble and the two irate old men were persuaded to part company and go their own ways, but it was to be some time before they spoke to each other again.

It must be said that, after a while, Osla saw the funny side of things and was heard to say that had the rascals who made up the story picked a more congenial man the outcome might have been very different. She would never, she vowed, ever entertain the idea of living in such a desolate and barren place as the Wast Neeps or with such a witless and crabbit old man.

For his part Tirval never mentioned the affair except to state that when he discovered the miscreant who started such a scandalous and malicious rumour, he, Tirval, would soon settle his hash.

Peace having been declared amongst us boys, the weekend was to be spent camping and great funs were in store. Someone had found some old linoleum which was soon spread on the tent floor to keep us off the possibly wet grass.

So, that weekend there were several of us ready and willing to spend lots of time camping. Our interest in cowboys of the American West meant that we were avid followers of such programmes on radio and in the pages of the comics we read. It also made us very adept in the usage of the lingo often found therein.

We were very cheerful as we gathered in the tent that night: Hamish, Billy, John Williamson, Basil and myself. We had intended to go right to sleep but as ever on those occasions our excitement kept us awake and chatty.

Basil and myself were lying nearest to the door end, and in the fading daylight inside the tent I looked at the blanket covered bodies around me before remarking to Basil, "I hope nobody snores too loud."

"If they do," Basil said sleepily, "we'll just have to head 'em off at the Pass and corral them outside."

"Shut up, you two, an' go ta sleep," Hamish growled.

"Or we'll fill you full o' lead an' dump you outside," that was Billy.

"I'm not ready for the boneyard yet," was our duetted reply.

"You blinkin'-well soon will be if you don't shut up," Hamish retorted with feeling.

The only sound to follow that was a burst of laughter from the other John and Billy. Basil and I were keeping our heads well down as we lay sniggering into our blankets.

Late that night something moved in the darkness beyond the tent and those of us still in a half awake state pulled the blankets over our heads as we heard the 'something' circle the tent. This was especially true of those in the most vulnerable positions near the door.

Daa was there at first light urging us to get out of our beds and not lie there sleeping like a lot of lazy-bones. We didn't pay much attention to him, but we did discover that there had been at least two prowlers in the night ... Daa, and Billy and Basil's father had both come out to check that we were all right and maybe give us a little bit of a scare too.

We did get out of the tent very quickly that morning, not because of Daa's early morning call, but because the tent was simply crawling with forkietails.

We could only agree that the forkietails had probably been in the lino before it was spread on the floor of the tent. We decided to abandon our campsite for a little while and seek something more interesting to do ... we would return later and if necessary move the tent away from the site of the forkietail invasion.

Chapter Eleven

The Half-Barrel

The old pier at Ravensgeo was not a very safe place for children to play and our grandfather was often ordering us away from the structure. Of course, we didn't think we were in any danger, but before our time, two boys had lost their lives in the area and Daa had no wish for the same to happen to any of us.

Still, the beaches on either side of the pier were reasonably harmless, unless we ventured too far out in the sea, which we were sometimes apt to do. It is strange that we were willing to take so many risks with the sea, when neither Hamish nor myself ever learned to swim.

I cannot recall which one of us found the half-barrel, but as soon as we saw it we realised that it would be almost like having a little boat and was something we could make real use of.

We decided that if we attached a rope to it and put some stones in for ballast, one of us could sit in it and be pulled along the shallows, which was fine for the one being towed, but not so enjoyable for those doing the pulling. There was also the problem of waar-lined rocks into which the barrel would bump and stick, giving the one inside a jolt and those pulling some hard work to get it loose again. There was no long clear haul where the half-barrel could go for any distance without hitting something hard and immovable.

True, we could have let it drift out as far as the rope would reach, but in that case it only took those on the rope to let go, and the barrel, complete with a very frightened boy, would head out for the middle of the voe. We reasoned that once such a thing happened the barrel would very likely capsize once it came to larger waves, thereby spilling the unfortunate boy into the water, from which it would be very doubtful if he would escape.

Some other way had to be found to give us a good length of

sailing or towing time and it was then that someone came up with a really daring plan. A rope, he said, could be attached to the pier at Ravensgeo and then taken along the beach to where the pier stood at Gardiestaing, and attached there. Then the half-barrel could be pulled between the two. Our only problem with this was in the length of rope required, as the piers were some distance apart.

However, it was impossible to do it at that moment for the tide was coming in and it was only when it was out that we could get far enough along the Ravensgeo pier to make it worthwhile. The thing to do now was to find enough suitable rope to stretch the distance.

We did not even wonder if such a plan was dangerous or not, and I've no doubt that given time we would have found enough rope and attempted to pull one another across over deep water ... it was a tragedy waiting to happen.

However, our guardian angel was watching over us in the form of Old Daa. The next day when we hurried down to the beach the half-barrel has disappeared.

"It must have been Old Bowe," someone said disgustedly.

"Yeah," Hamish replied, "he was lik'ly frightened it sank wi' one o' us in it. He's always worryin' what we get up to an' I saw him watchin' us yesterday."

"Maybe we could find it again," I said, "an' use it while he's no' lookin'."

"Don't be silly," Hamish said, looking disgusted, "he'll have hidden it too well."

"Lik'ly he sank it in deep water," Basil said.

We turned then and stared at the stretch of sea between the piers. We had put stones in the barrel for ballast so all he had to do was put a few more in and let it sink. Personally, I doubt if it had suffered that fate, as it seems to me to be a waste of a good half-barrel at a time when such things had many uses, but whatever happened to it our plan of using it in such a dangerous way came to an abrupt end.

We did ask Daa if he had seen it but he would not admit to taking it away though we were pretty sure it had to be him. We did not think of the fact that it might have been reclaimed by whoever owned it. Perhaps one of the bakeries was using it to store things in. We even made a few visits to the bakeries to see if we could spot it, but although we were greeted kindly and given a handful of raisins to eat we failed to spot anything that looked like our half-barrel.

"I doubt it's where you'll never find it," was Daa's only comment.

Life in the 1950s was not all fishing and fun and for most grown-ups it was often back-breaking labour, an example of which came round each year at peat cutting time. This was a task that had to be done if you wanted to have a warm fire in winter ... to buy coal was an unthinkable and unnecessary extravagance.

The long hours of summer daylight gave a good chance of working late into the evenings, which must have been a boon to those who worked at daytime jobs and only had evenings and weekends free for the peats. Of course, there were always neighbours willing to help and in return you helped them.

The first thing to be done when starting on your peat bank was to 'fley' it. This entailed the removal of the heathery turf to expose the peat. Then came the really hard work of cutting out the peat with a tool called a 'tushkar' and in time there would be enough peat cut to last over the next winter and spring.

These days people are concerned about the destruction of the remaining peat moors of Britain and have every right to be so, but there is a great difference between some company stripping the moors bare with machines and the crofter cutting some for his fire. After all, crofters have been doing that since the islands were first settled without depleting peat stocks much. There are, however, few people working peats these days as other forms of heating have come to the islands in recent years. Back in the early fifties though we loved being at the peat hill and, when not helping our elders, would play about the hill or hunt for 'heather berries', the small, glossy, purple crowberry, usually ripe in August.

That year we had missed the 'casting' or digging out of the peats, when they were laid out in rows to dry and left until it was considered time to 'raise' them. To do this they were set up on end, leaning against each other looking just like dozens of little tepees, so

Daa proudly displays twin lambs.

that the air could blow all around them and finish the drying process. Raising peats was much more lively and interesting as some of the women folk would be there too, and the whole operation was done in a lighter and more cheerful way with much good-natured banter and laughter. This despite the hordes of midges determined to make our lives as miserable as possible.

We enjoyed the 'raising' and would help with the peats where we could, but we did have plenty of time to roam about looking for berries or just playing in the hill. Sooner or later, though, we would sit down to eat something, and on the day I recall we had just settled down to our feast when Hamish suddenly slapped his leg, shouting, "Yaah." The word was just out of his mouth when I felt something bite my leg just above the sock. It was my turn to cry out and slap my leg. Uncle John laughed and called over, "Mooritoogs got you boys?"

We jumped up then, brushing the furiously biting ants off ourselves.

"Blinkin' mooritoogs!" we cried.

It gave our elders a laugh and taught us a lesson: when sitting down to eat in the hill be sure you are not sitting on an ant's nest.

The hill could be a dangerous place for the unwary as there were many boggy areas, but we were kept well away from them. There was a story, possibly quoted as a warning to us, about a Minister of the Church who was moving house from one parish in Yell to another. His flitting was done by horse and cart sometime in the 16th century. The cart, piled high with his belongings, was trundling along nicely when he decided to take a shortcut he had been told about. In no time at all he found the horse, cart, and himself slipping into a bog. The poor man could do nothing but sit on his seat on the cart and watch as they sank slowly deeper. Luckily for him those who were helping him to flit came along in time to rescue him, but the poor old horse and the cartload of furniture and belongings sank down into the bog and were never seen again.

Another day we were taken back to the hill by Daa as he was going to 'roog' the peats. This meant to build them into a heap as near to the road as possible.

In the old days peats would either be carried home in a 'kishie' (a straw basket slung onto the back), or would be taken home by pony. Daa had peats near the shore at the head of the voe and it was these we intended to 'roog' this morning. We were busy gathering the peats for Daa to stack when, suddenly, Hamish looked over at me and called, "Mind your feet, John, yon's the trow's grave you're standin' on."

I had clean forgotten about the Windhouse trow and now stood for a few moments staring down at my feet half expecting to see the trow glowering up at me. It was only Daa's voice that stirred me into movement, "Come awa' frae there, boy," he ordered. Like many of the locals he was wary of the place. Not frightened, but just a little uneasy.

"I was just fetchin' peats," I said lamely, as I carried my load over to him.

"I wonder what's in the trow's grave?" Hamish said.

"Boy," Daa said sharply, "some things are best no' questioned."

Hamish did not reply but shrugged his shoulders and began gathering peats again. I wondered if he'd made that comment just to see what reaction came from our grandfather. Whatever, as we gathered our fuel I kept well away from the raised area known as the 'trow's grave'.

Then came the day that Uncle John, Hamish and myself set out for the same place to bag up some peats which Daa would come and take home in the old black boat.

We had been working for a while before we saw the boat approaching the beach. They had timed everything for when the tide was in and the boat could come almost to the peat bank. The bags were duly filled, tied up to prevent peats from slipping out and set at the top of the beach from where they could easily be loaded aboard. When enough were done we stopped and John and Daa loaded the boat.

Daa had already got the mast and the square sail rigged up, for with the bags of peat piled high in her there would be no room to use the oars.

I had been thinking that with such a cargo we would have to walk home with Uncle John but I was wrong. When she was all loaded up we boys were lifted aboard and told to sit very still as, with John attending to the sail, Daa steered us back to the noost at Ravensgeo.

We boys felt we had been on a real adventure but it was almost the end of the peats for that year as the next time we would be taking the main load home by lorry. Of course, then there were more people involved and the lorry would make two trips before all the peats were home. Then John and Daa would build them into a large stack outside the house ready for use when required.

I think everyone sighed with relief to know that the 'peat hill' was finished for another year. We boys, however, regretted that we would get no more rides on top of a swaying load of peats ... that had been great fun.

Daa always ran a few sheep out on the hill and would go to check them regularly. That year, one of his ewes had produced twin lambs, which had really pleased him. Lambs were usually kept in the fields beside the house until old enough to be let loose in the hills. Sometimes too, the lambie house which stood a little way in front of the house, would have weaker lambs and their mothers sheltering there until they were strong enough to survive in the outside world.

One day, just after our escapade with the barrel, I was called upon to go to Brown's shop for some items of urgently required foodstuff. I would rather just have gone across the road to the Ravensgeo shop but after being told which shop to go to I didn't like to tempt fate by going somewhere else.

Upon my return I discovered Hamish was missing.

"Where's Hamish gone?" I asked.

"I think he's gone up over to Gardie to speak with Billy and Jim Gray," was the reply.

"Oh," I said, thinking that he might have waited for me.

Daa appeared in the doorway just then to say that he was going up the hill to look at the sheep.

"Take John Arnold with you," Aunt Bertha said, "Hamish has gone and left him so he's kinda at a loss for something to do."

So that is how I came to be tagging along with Daa that day. Unlike the time I went to the whelks with Uncle John, we called along houses in Gardie on the way. We did not even go up to the road but went along by the front of the houses visiting people as we went. They were all related to us anyway so we knew them well.

This being the way of things our journey was delayed at each house as Daa yarned with the inhabitants. Only Billy and Basil's parents were not at home. We spent some time speaking to Johnnie Andrew Guthrie, Granny Katie's brother. Her father had been married twice and there were nineteen in her family so it was not surprising that some lived locally. Therefore, it was some time before we arrived at Gardie Ness, the last house, to find Willie (Daa's brother) and Allie, his wife, busy outside in their yard. With them was Jeannie Ratter (Granny Katie's sister), whose husband Tammie we had just left. With three of them to talk to Daa delayed longer there. I just tried my best to avoid too much attention though I answered shyly when they spoke directly to me.

How glad I was to be away over the fence and out on the hill again. They were nice people but I was very easily embarrassed at that age and preferred to either be on my own or with someone I knew very well.

That day we went down by the krö and over the brig that crossed Laxa Burn to follow the burn up the hill. Daa stopped every little while to gaze around him checking even the most distant sheep to decide to whom they belonged.

To me all sheep looked much alike, except that some were light and others dark, or somewhere in between, but to Daa they were all individuals and he could tell you who owned each animal.

I loved being up the hill, especially along Laxa Burn and the hill of Setter. With Daa making frequent stops to check sheep I had plenty time to inspect the burn, search for trout and do pretty much as I wanted, as long as I kept an eye on Daa so that I didn't begin to lag behind.

I'd always been a bit of a dreamer: even in a crowd of people I'd be able to shut off and think my own thoughts. Sitting there on a heathery knowe, waiting whilst my companion studied some distant yowes, I thought how the hillsides on each side of the burn would look lovely with trees along their length. I doubt if, at that time, I'd seen a tree taller than ten feet and even the willow outside the porch didn't get higher than that. However, I somehow knew they should be birch trees ... I only learned years later that at one time this part of Yell was covered with birch woods.

After going for some distance up along the burn Daa decided that his sheep were all doing very well and we turned for home again.

On the following day, Hamish, Jim and Billy really got themselves into trouble. On a visit to one of the bakeries the three boys had been given an almost empty tin of extract of malt. When they became tired of sampling it they cast about to find another use for it and their eyes fell on the outhouse that stood some distance from the main house.

There was no indoor plumbing in Yell at that time so there was a great need for such buildings and now the boys were struck by the idea that our grandfather would soon be paying the outhouse a visit. Clutching the tin, Hamish led Jim and Billy to the house where they stayed only long enough to smear the extract of malt over the seat.

They knew they would be in trouble once Daa learned what they had done but were pretty sure that in the end he would laugh it off as a boyish prank and make them clean the mess up ... imagine their surprise and consternation when instead of Daa, Auntie Bertha came out of the house and headed for the toilet!

They knew she would not let them off with their prank without a great deal of trouble for them. As soon as they were sure where she was going they made themselves scarce and tried to keep out of her way until she'd calmed down some. That night I felt that I was the 'good' peerie boy for a change and I was very thankful not to be one of the culprits.

Having the outside toilet at some distance from the house meant that it was a cold and gloomy place to visit on a dark winter's night, neither was it very welcoming on a summer night when the wind howled and rain spattered in your face.

One day, Hamish and Billy were playing on forbidden ground ... namely our grandfather's vegetable patch, the kailyard. Presently they were joined by Jim and the three boys were having fun. Then suddenly, out from the house sallied an enraged Old Daa. This time they had gone too far and he was determined to sort them out.

Jim and Billy took off for the far fence at a run but Hamish dropped to the ground as soon as Daa appeared and lay amongst the kail stocks, hidden by the large leaves. Daa now entered the yard in pursuit of the fleeing boys not realising the ringleader was lying only a few feet away from him.

Hamish, watching Daa's feet approach, moved carefully out of his way but when Daa came abreast of him he surged forward in a daring tackle, which took his grandfather completely by surprise and caused him to measure his length amongst his own cabbages. It was said later that Daa's fall ruined far more plants than we boys would have done for in a whole season.

Once again I was not one of those who was in trouble but, needless to say, I was included in the ban that put Daa's kailyard out of bounds for the foreseeable future.

Another time the same boys found some wood and decided to build themselves a raft. For several days they worked on the project, well away from Daa's protective gaze, out along the beach below Gardie Ness. At last the time came when their craft was finished but, alas, the day was so well spent that they decided to head for their respective homes and leave the launching of their fine vessel until the next morning.

After a night, possibly spent in dreams of derring-do on the high seas, they met up and hurried down to the beach. Imagine their surprise and disgust when all they found there was the wood ... not a raft any more as someone had come along in the night and taken their fine craft apart again.

It was then that they realised that Willie Leask, who lived in Gardie Ness, might just be as protective towards them as his brother was, but they never really found out for sure which one had undone all their work.

The holidays would soon be coming to an end and we would return to the little house by the Pool. Still, there was a week or two to go yet and I had no doubt that in the time left to us we would have plenty of funs and times of enjoyment.

Chapter Twelve

Farewell to Yell

The day of the Mid Yell Regatta dawned with a light breeze and an almost cloud-free sky. The voe was a fine place for holding sailing races though our main interest lay in what was happening on shore where the sports and entertainments were held at Linkshouse.

There were a number of races for both children and grown-ups: egg and spoon, three-legged and the sack race to name but three. I had no intention of entering for any, though I'd taken part in the years when we lived in Mid Yell, but I was soon roped in for something and great fun was had by all.

For a while we watched the sailing races. The vessels competing were the Shetland fourareen (four-oared), built on the lines of the Norse galleys but minus the high dragonhead prows and sternposts. There was a variety of races in or on the sea including those sailing races so much enjoyed by those who took part. Daa and Uncle John sometimes took part in the square-sail race, which was about the only race the old boat stood any chance in. Then there would be swimming races and diving, which were fine to watch, but certainly not for us non-swimmers to take part in.

It was a day of much enjoyment and would be followed in the evening by a concert and dance. Hamish would be singing at the concert as he was often asked to sing on such occasions. I was pleased to leave that kind of thing to him as I would have disliked having to perform before so many people, even if I'd had a good voice.

When evening came we were eager to get to the hall and couldn't wait to get into our seats so that the show could start. It was always interesting to watch the hall fill up with people whom you hardly recognised because they were all dressed up for the evening.

After what we considered an extremely long wait, the lights were dimmed, the stage curtains drawn back and our evening's entertainment began.

There were quite a few musical items and a sketch or two. Hamish came on and sang popular songs. I noticed that when he began to sing the whole audience went silent and I realised they were listening so intently that you could almost have heard a pin drop. What a pity that tape-recorders had not made it to Yell by then. Strangely, there are no known recordings of him singing during the years of his childhood.

When the concert was over all the seats had to be taken up to make the room ready for dancing. Seats were left along the walls where people could sit when not dancing. Unlike the village halls of today, there were no bars, no people spending their time sitting at tables drinking instead of dancing, and all the people there were of one mind ... they were going to enjoy themselves and dance the night away.

Although most women of the time did not go into bars, and would have been very embarrassed had they been caught drinking at a dance, most men came to the hall well-supplied and spent some time partaking in liquid refreshment outside the hall. Some men often cached their supply of liquor near the hall only to have some of it disappear when some young lads discovered it and got high as kites on VP wine and black rum.

Inside the hall we children caused something like pandemonium with our wild charging about the floor, sliding, jumping, running and generally making a din. If it seemed that we were becoming too excited then one of our aunts would 'have a few words with us' and the threat of being taken home again did work for a few minutes.

At last the dancing would begin and some children would join in and dance properly. For me, however, dancing was the least important thing and I would be content to watch or wander about the hall seeing what was going on.

After a while there would be a break for tea, sandwiches and biscuits. First would come the cups, carried around the hall in zinc baths, then would come the tea in large kettles, followed by the food ... I had a very enjoyable time.

The dance often went on until the early hours but this time our presence there was not destined to be for long.

There was nothing Daa liked better than a good fun and he did enjoy an occasional dram. On this evening he had been outside with the other men having something a little stronger than tea and at last it was thought someone should take him home. This was the first and only time I ever saw Daa the worse for drink.

The job of taking him home fell to Uncle John who was in a more sober frame of mind. We bairns went with them, closely followed by at least one aunt. The thing that stands out clearly in my mind is that Daa sang all the way home, except for the few times he paused to reprimand his son for getting in his way and holding his arm too firmly.

"Has anybody here seen Kelly?" rang out loud and clear over the still, calm night that held the island in its grip. I am sure that the words would have been clearly heard right over to North-a-Voe.

Our idea had been to return to the hall with Uncle John but we were in for a surprise. Rose and I were told that it was now bedtime for us. Hamish, being my senior by two and a half years, was allowed to return but us younger ones were heading for bed with many a tearful "It's not fair," on the way.

I did not witness the next story though it happened in the years when we holidayed in Yell. This time the shoe was on the other foot and it was Uncle John who had taken too much liquid enjoyment at a dance. Daa, finding that his son was in no fit state to walk home did the best he could ... he fetched a wheelbarrow, put the alcoholically disabled one in it, and set out for home.

He had trundled the barrow about halfway when his supposedly slumbering son popped up his head, looked up at him and, with the exaggerated preciseness of the drunk, said, "Faider, stop you now an' let me out 'til I give you a spell."

Unfortunately his father's reply has not been recorded.

There were often families of tinkers who spent much of the summer in or near Mid Yell and they often came around trying to sell their wares. They made some fine tin whistles which we tried to buy from them if we had enough pennies.

Often they had a forceful selling technique, especially should they find the woman of the house at home alone. A story was told of how one woman got the better of two of them one day by using an even more forceful argument.

This lady and her parents lived at a fair distance from the neighbouring crofts and, on the day in question, the parents had left the house early to go to a sale some distance away leaving the daughter at home to do the chores.

Suddenly she beheld two tinker men approaching the house. Wisely she decided to meet them outside and, after the pleasantries of greeting were over, the two, thinking they would easily browbeat her into buying, set out to make a sale.

Arms akimbo, she refused even to entertain the idea of buying anything. However, at her refusal they only became more determined to sell her something. She listened politely until she began to lose her temper at which point she cried, "I've told you, I don't want to buy any of your wares and I want you to leave. NOW."

"Och, but lady ... " one began, only to be interrupted.

"If you don't leave right now I'll go and fetch the rifle and shoot the pair of you ... and I'm not joking."

They thought that idea was very amusing and fell about laughing. Possibly they didn't believe the woman knew the first thing about guns and they stood there laughing as she turned and disappeared into the house. However, when they saw her come back out the door expertly loading a rifle they took fright and hastily gathered up their wares and fled. As they ran out the gate and down the hillside one shouted to the other, "See here, ma man, you run one way an' I'll run the other ... she can't shoot us both!"

The story does not tell whether the woman fired any shots or not but it is doubtful if those two tinkers ever went near that croft again.

One of the most exciting times was when everyone gathered to 'caa' (drive) the sheep to the krö to be 'rooed' and dipped.

Shetland sheep have the kind of coat that does not need clipping and to 'roo' simply means to pull the wool off.

There were men, women, children and dogs all shouting, whistling or making some noise and, of course, the sheep themselves were baaing as they were driven down the hillsides by the dogs. To be truthful it seemed to me that some of the dogs understood sheep far better than the humans who were shouting orders to them. Some of the men had tin 'tinker' whistles, which they blasted away on every now and then.

It appeared that while both men and women were becoming flushed and overheated from their physical exertion, the dogs were, except for the occasional burst of barking, much more silent and seemed to be enjoying themselves more. Very likely they had looked forward to this event with far more anticipation than their two-legged counterparts.

At last, though, all the sheep would be in the krö and the rooing could begin. Sheep would be grabbed with rough but experienced hands, stripped of their wool, dipped and released. They would run a little distance, bleating like mad, stop, shake themselves and look back at the proceedings as if wondering why humans acted in this strange way.

I would think that sheep were not, perhaps, as stupid as most people thought them to be and I was convinced that really they enjoyed all this rough and tumble. Probably they thought humans were working for them by removing their heavy winter coats and leaving them nice and cool during what was left of the summer.

Sometimes tempers would fray and disagreements build up into open hostilities. There was a lot of teasing which could upset people with a more underdeveloped sense of humour, but for much of the time there was interesting talk, much laughter and camaraderie, and by the end of the day old friendships might have deepened and new ones been forged ... aye, and more than one couple likely met for the first time at the krö.

Now our holiday was fast coming to an end but there was one treat left for us. On the last Sunday we were all going for a picnic to one of the islands just outside Mid Yell Voe. Our destination was either Kay Holm, or the much larger Hascosay. The latter island had once been inhabited and we had been told stories about some events that had once happened there including the tale of the wreck of the *Krageroe*.

This happened in 1803. The vessel was on a voyage between London and Tonsberg in Norway when she was caught in a storm and lost her main mast. With great difficulty they managed to get into the shelter of the island of Whalsay, where both crew and passengers went on shore leaving the ship anchored off the island.

Then, in the middle of the night, the cable snapped and the *Krageroe* drifted north to meet her end on the spume-rimmed rocks of Hascosay. However, she was seen by people on Yell and Fetlar, who hurried to launch their boats and, despite the heavy swell left by the storm, set out for Hascosay. By the time the ship hit the rocks there were already thirty people on the island eager to gather the bits of her.

Over the next few days people came from Unst, Fetlar and Yell, and even parts of the north mainland, until there was nothing left of the ship. The Admiral's Depute of Yell, Mr Hoseason, from Aywick, went with two men in an attempt to stop the plundering, but they were outnumbered and, although they managed to save some things, much of the wooden vessel disappeared.

At the time there were three houses on the island inhabited by families called Sinclair, Stove and Hughson. These people, whilst helping the authorities by storing items in their own homes, were later accused of plundering the wreck.

There were many such stories about the islands and thankfully some of them were written down and are still with us today, but so many must have been lost over the years.

We had been on picnics in other years when our parents were also there. How a dozen people managed to get into Daa's old boat without her sinking I don't know. This time, however, there were only about nine of us so there was a little more room. The day was calm, the sun shone and everything was quiet as the boat crept away from the pier and turned its bow towards the mouth of the voe.

Over the land it was beginning to be warm, so much so that

even the birds seemed to be conserving their energy, but out over the voe there was a fresher feel about the day with the tiniest breeze caused by the movement of the boat.

"Boy, stop yon," Daa said, as I tried to grab some lucky-lines, "an' sit still."

I did as ordered and tried to be as still as I could but it is most difficult to be still when there are so many interesting things to see and the seawater was a strong draw for fingers that longed to be wet. It was not to be the only time I was reprimanded on that short voyage.

It was the grown-ups who decided, much to our delight, to row into the caves in the cliffs at the Head of Hevdagarth. I liked going in there for we could look down into the clear water and see the bottom.

"Look," cried Rose, gazing down into the sea, "you can see skadiman's heads."

I looked down and saw several sea urchins on the rocky bottom.

"Wouldn't it be lovely if we could reach down and touch them?" I said.

I don't think she liked that idea because she pulled a face and said, "I've touched one we found on the beach, John Arnold, an' they're rough an' cold an' prickly, but they are pretty from up here."

"There's a crab," I said, "an' sillocks! See over there." But before she could look the little fish disappeared under the boat, but she saw the peerie white crab and leaned over to get a better view.

"Now, Rose," cautioned one of our aunts, "don't lean out over the side. And John Arnold, keep your hands out of the water or maybe the crabs will catch your fingers."

"They can't," I retorted, "they're far too far down in the sea."

We did not stay in the cave long as I think the cliffs above and around us were a bit overpowering for some of the ladies. After that it was only a short row to Kay Holm.

As we landed, I asked, "Are we going to Hascosay too?"

"Get yoursel' ashore," said Uncle John, "I doubt if we'll have time for more than here."

Kay Holm was a rock lined little island without the stretches of sandy beaches that its larger neighbour had, but it had some interesting bits of topography, at least to us bairns, and leaving our elders to the task of bringing our picnic things ashore we set out to explore. Sometimes there would be seals lying on the rocks that we could watch. We had often been warned not to go too near to seals for if we disturbed them suddenly, and made them feel cut off from the sea, they were apt to snap at you.

Dad told us about one he and some of his pals found on the beach when he was a boy. It was unmoving and looked to be quite dead, but when Dad went up and poked at it with a short stick it suddenly burst into action and, had he been slightly slower in jumping away, he could have lost his hand as well as his stick. After that he was always more wary of creatures that looked to be dead on the beach.

Whatever, any seals we saw that day were well out in the water, but as we played and climbed amongst the rocks we saw a neesik or two break surface between the two islands blowing air. Then we were called back to the picnic site and all thoughts of seals and neesiks were forgotten as we tucked into our picnic food.

All in all we had a really fine day. When the picnic was over we were left to range the island again and it wasn't long before we found our way down to the beach where we spent our time searching for sea creatures along the rocky, sea-weedy shoreline.

The grown-ups relaxed in the summer sun, but either Daa or Uncle John kept their eyes on where we were and what we were doing. They knew from past experience that we might do something silly ... should we find wood or something ... e.g. half-barrels ... we would, without doubt, be in or on them, trying to race each other round the island.

That special day came to an end all too soon and we were a little saddened to be in the boat again heading for home. Yet a few days later, when we at last said farewell to Mid Yell, we were looking forward to returning to the Pool and our parents. Of course, we were sorry to part from our family and friends and would spend the next year longing to return.

Daa was to come down with us and he was all ready to go to

catch the bus at least an hour before the appointed time. He was impatiently stamping about, both inside and outside, looking for the hundredth time at the sky, trying to judge what the weather was going to do; then inside again to glare at the clock and ask if we intended to go home today or not, telling us that if we didn't hurry up we would miss the bus and be in real trouble from our parents.

After I'd finished breakfast I wandered outside, and on my way to the little house that had had its seat malted just a few weeks earlier, I paused to gaze once more on the voe. Between me and the beach stood the old lambie house where everything Daa needed found a home. Also in the building were housed any lambs which might be in need of shelter and extra care. One end was used as a pigeon house, the other as a henhouse. Rose enjoyed going to the pigeon end when Daa was feeding and it was the kind of place that drew our attention like a magnet. It would only take us to see Daa or John heading in that direction to have us going after them.

It would be a long time before we returned. To a child a year seems to be a very long time. Slowly, with a sad shake of my head, I continued on my way ... thankfully there was no malt on the seat that morning.

Chapter Thirteen

Tryshtsom Times

Upon our arrival home one of the first tasks we were given was to go to Sumburgh Farm and fetch Sheila as she had been there whilst we'd been away. This meant going around the Pool, over the airport runway and on past Jarlshof, the old Pictish and Norse settlement. I don't recall us having much interest in the old ruins, but then we were intent on being reunited with Sheila.

Guess who nearly hit the roof when we walked in? She went wild with excitement but had calmed down a little by the time we set out on our homeward journey. As we walked across the sand dunes she went racing off amongst the grassy sand only to reappear a little later with a live, but very wild (and angry) rabbit in her jaws.

This unfortunate creature soon found itself removed from her mouth only to be firmly placed inside a boy's jacket, where it would stay until we arrived home then be put into the run with our two tame rabbits.

Sheila certainly had a very soft mouth, for when we arrived home with the rabbit Dad took the animal and searched its fur for any signs of damage on its skin, but found not a scratch. We were so pleased to have a dog that did not harm what it caught. We were inclined to think that the rabbit had been a gift from her for coming to fetch her ... she saw the rabbit and thought, 'Oh, the bairns would like one of you'.

Needless to say, by the next morning the tame ones were still in the run, but the visitor had gone.

Hamish was still in great demand for concerts and was to win a prize for his singing at the Shetland Music Festival. Another time, he toured Shetland with the great Scottish tenor, Robert Wilson, who hoped to take him south on a tour of Scotland, but this fell through as Hamish was considered too young for such an adventure.

Aunt Bertha Anderson in North Roe.

When he was singing on the Shetland mainland we would sometimes attend the concert and dance, which we enjoyed greatly, though, to be sure, I would not be dancing at them. Even if I enjoyed being in the company of young ladies I had no wish to dance with one ... not yet.

News came one day that Aunt Bertha had been taken to hospital suffering from diabetes and was now in a coma. It was a bad time and one Saturday we were taken up to Lerwick as our mother wished to visit her sister. Whilst she was in the hospital we waited outside on the pavement.

It was not an experience we enjoyed and to me there seemed to be far too many vehicles about. Here there was no soft sand or green grass and the buildings were much too close together for my liking. Little did I know that in a few years I would be happily sledging down by the hospital as if I'd never spent a winter anywhere else.

Thankfully, Aunt Bertha recovered and in time was to marry and settle in North Roe, which meant that there was another area for us to explore on the Shetland mainland.

Behind our house there were some old lengths of wood lying doing nothing so we decided to put them to use as our 'ship'. We had many bold adventures and daring raids on that old pirate ship. True, she did not look much like a ship, but to us she was the *Queen of the Seas*, sailing to lands of golden sands and swaying palms; fighting storms, raging seas, wild natives, other pirates and, of course, the Spanish on the Main.

Tommy, our neighbour, ploughing or harvesting the field above our house, must have had many a lightsome moment when he saw some of our swashbuckling antics as we sailed our good ship through an imaginary storm.

We had a very bold and fearless captain and crew: Hamish the captain, myself as mate, and Rose, and any of our other pals, as crew. Sometimes too, the other children of the neighbourhood would become the attacking enemy, and Eastshore, Virkie would resound to the din of our battle. But such a shore bound vessel would never do for our adventurous captain after having had the excitement of days out in Daa's old boat, and the idea was forming in his mind ... what about building a 'real ship' that we could sail around on the Pool? The attempt to build a raft had been severely sabotaged in Mid Yell, but here in the shallow waters of the Pool it was unlikely that anyone would object.

Whilst Rose and I were still satisfied to play at being sailors on a few pieces of wood behind the house, Hamish had arrived at an age where playing such games was not enough, and was something he was beginning to consider too childish for a boy of his age ... he was now a teenager.

When the weather was fine we spent more time in the Pool than we did on dry land. Early on we had invented spears made from a long shaft of wood, with a six or four-inch nail sharpened to a needle like point and attached to the end of the shaft. With these deadly weapons we hunted 'flooks' (flounders) when the tide was in.

Our method was simple: barefoot we would move slowly along until we felt a fish under our toes. Then down went the spears with some force ... how we didn't spear our toes I'll never know.

Sometimes finding the wooden shaft could be a problem. Broom handles were ideal but Lord help the boy who knocked the head off his mother's broom and claimed the handle. Once a shaft was found all that was then required was for the boy to cut a groove for the nail and bind it on.

Another way of catching flooks was perhaps a little less dangerous. It involved digging large holes in the sand when the tide was out then waiting until it came in and went out again. A visit to the holes would then supply us with several fine flatfish. With the first method we might not have speared our toes, but other injuries did happen ... at least they did to me.

One Sunday, cousin James John, his wife and family came to visit as they had been to see his father just along the road, then came to spend some time with us. We were playing on the beach but were called on to come up to the house and set off from the beach at a run. I was last in the race and as I ran through the long grass I felt the sharp bite of something slice through the skin between the toes on my left foot. By the time I arrived at the door there was a trail of red in my wake. The cut, probably done by the edge of a blade of grass, required expert attention and a doctor was sent for.

That run through the long grass earned me three weeks off school, but more permanent damage had been done too – a nerve had been severed and ever after I couldn't bear anything between those toes.

However, I was to have a worse accident than that one election day when a car came to pick mother up and take her to vote. She had no great wish to go and leave us alone, but the car was there and the whole operation would only take five or ten minutes. The next-door house was only a short distance away ... we would be safe enough.

Before she left she warned us not to play in the but end where she had been boiling water. She left us in no doubt that we would be in severe trouble if she discovered we had been near the fire while she was out.

Rose and I were throwing a ball or something to each other and were soon in the but end. As the play became wilder I dived ever nearer the stove to catch the thrown object. Rose was further away, more out toward the door. Suddenly my jacket caught the pan of newly boiled water knocking it off the stove to spill its contents over

With East Shore visitors – Back: Mary Leask, Georgina Strachan, Tammie Strachan, Andrew Leask. Front: Sheila, John Arnold and Rose.

my left foot.

I screamed in agony and danced around on one leg as I urged Rose to run to our neighbour for help.

"Fetch Isa," I wailed, meaning the lady next door, but as I spoke the pain left my foot. "It's all right," I gasped, "it's not sore now."

Rose paused, worry and apprehension on her face, as she watched me remove my shoe. I still felt no pain, but as I began to remove the sock and saw the skin of my foot come with it, I cried, "It's not all right. Go an' fetch Isa."

Rose ran, but I can't recall whether Isa or Mum arrived first.

Whatever, the doctor was called and I was in bed again and off school for another three weeks ... missing school bothered me not in the least and there was one good thing to come out of all my pain.

One day, our good neighbour Isa brought me a present ... a tiny kitten. I called her June and the little bundle of white and tabby fur soon became a dear friend. She was the only cat I managed to train to come to me, and follow me around when I snapped my fingers, and that without the enticement of titbit rewards.

Every winter I was terribly troubled by chilblains on the backs of my fingers, which became open sores whenever the weather became cold. This meant that winter was not my happiest season although it would have taken a lot more than sore fingers to keep me inside when it was snowy.

One splendid snowy Saturday I followed Hamish and Rose out of the house as we ran to play with the other children of the neighbourhood. As we went, I heard Mum shout for me to come back to put on my warm knitted gloves, but nothing was going to delay the start of my fun in the snow if I could help it, so I pretended not to hear my mother's shouts and ran on.

We were playing up the hill behind the Garrick's house. To start with we had a fine snowball fight with the Garrick girls, Kathleen, Anna and Ruby, which soon became like a blizzard as we all began throwing snow around. After that my hands were never idle; rolling snowballs, building snowmen, steering sledges and trying to build igloos. So, what if the snow I touched was tinged with blood sometimes? That was the price I was more than willing to pay for such a day of enjoyment.

"Just look at your hands," Mum cried when we reluctantly returned home, "they are just blue wi' cold ... and see the state of them! Couldn't you have come home for your gloves?"

I looked at my hands and they certainly were cold. The back of each finger was a red open wound, but I felt no pain.

"It's okay," I grinned, "they're no' sore."

"John Arnold!" she exclaimed in disbelief. "They must be! Why, they are just red raw!"

Surprising as it may seem, when the wounds healed this time

they were never to return. No matter how hard the frosts were, or how bitterly cold my hands became, the skin would never break open like that again. The question as to whether the snow or the cold did the healing is one I cannot answer, but something that day worked a small miracle on my hands and made a big difference to my life.

When our parents decided to keep poultry on a small scale the ideal place for them was our stone roofed gang hut and the area in front was fenced off as a hen run. This meant that we needed to find another gang hut, but where? At this time the rabbits were in the old wartime air raid shelter. We realised that while it was really far too big for two rabbits it would be just fine for our needs. I think that, perhaps, the rabbits were pleased to move into a normal sized hutch with a large run, and we were delighted to move our gang hut gear into the shelter ... needless to say we had some cleaning up to do first, for no matter how clean we'd kept the rabbits, they did leave a bit of a scent behind.

We seemed to be inundated with animal life at this time. Sheila had pups, Louise had kittens and sometimes we would take the rabbits into the house and let them all run together. There would also be times when we'd have a visit from one of our wild friends – a hedgehog that we would take in to have something to eat and a run about the floor with the rest of our group. How we laughed when Popeye, my black and white rabbit, bumped his nose into the hedgehog and jumped about a foot in the air with shock.

We were amazed when Sheila and Louise shared her kittens, and we wondered if kittens fed on dog's milk would bark instead of meow, but were told not to be silly and that the kittens would one day be a fine set of meowing cats ... but not in our house. Two cats in one house were more than enough for any family.

At the same time we were told that one dog was enough in a family and that we need not expect to keep one of the pups. However, one pup was to be sent up to Mid Yell so we could look after it until it was old enough to make the trip. Because he had spots on his head that looked to us like a face, we named him Dial and were sad when he left us, but happy to know he was up in Yell.

In past years we had taken tadpoles up to Yell and released them in the ditches near Ravensgeo. However, we never saw them again and suspected that Old Daa's ducks were partial to them, but there may yet be some frogs around Mid Yell whose ancestors dwelt in the more congenial ditches of southern Shetland. We housed several frogs in a large zinc bath outside the door ... until one night a violent and very determined feline creature managed to remove the netting wire cover and the frogs. This did, of course, break our hearts and had we known which of the cats around the place was the culprit they might have been in serious trouble.

When on the beach we were always on the look out for bottle

Aunt Mary Leask with Sheila.

messages, and we all found ones. Hamish wrote regularly to a girl called Jewel. Rose found a bottle message from a German fisherman or boy, Heinz, and I had found one from a girl called Mavis Hanson from West Hartlepool. I also wrote to a boy called John Donnan who once sent me a Christmas gift which I cherished: a book by Rutherford Montgomery called 'Iceblink'.

The work on Hamish's new vessel was coming along fine. Our father might make beautiful Shetland model yachts, up to five feet long, but Hamish was intent on making a raft that would sail in the shallow waters of the Pool. It might not be the most beautiful vessel afloat but it would be just what he'd always wanted ... his own command.

Admittedly, there was not much wood around in those days, but Hamish had managed to find enough to do the job, complete with broom handle mast. To be true, it was not made from the best of wood, and at least one of the boards was fairly rotten, but if you were careful where you put your feet it was quite safe to stand on the vessel.

Dad had once made a yacht from wreck wood and named her *The Wreck* but I think our new flagship fitted the name better. Though I don't recall that she was ever named ... she was just the 'Raft'.

Hamish laid orders on us younger ones that we were never to use the raft unless he was there and I don't think I ever went against that order. When he was there we often rafted around the Pool, but our mother had no wish for us to be going into danger on a few bits of doubtful wood ... how lucky we were that she never learned just how doubtful some of the wood really was.

About the time that Hamish was busy building the raft, Dad was working on one of the largest yachts he'd made. She must have been about five feet long with the look of a real winner about her. It was lovely to watch her turning from a few planks of wood into a sleek and beautiful craft under his expert hands.

This yacht was called *The Red Sea* and could have been sailing yet under that name had Dad not left her in a certain shed in Lerwick where other racing yachts were kept. One day, when he went to the shed to fetch her home, she had mysteriously disappeared ...

he was furious and we all wondered what had happened to her.

Sometimes we would be allowed to 'help' him work in the shed, but should we drop a tool or do something wrong he would raise one eyebrow and lower the other in a mock scowl and say, "Boy, you're as handy as the little bird they call the elephant!"

When I reached the age of twelve I had to go to another school and I liked that one as much as I liked any other. Here, in one of the classes, if a boy was just a little bit inattentive he was apt to be smacked across the ear with a twelve-inch wooden ruler, or startled out of his boots by having a wooden-backed blackboard duster thrown at him. It may be easy to tell that such a class was ruled by fear, and in such tense conditions a shy boy like myself could never do very good work. However, in other classes, taken in a more friendly atmosphere, I found some enjoyment. In the English class I lost myself in classic stories when the teacher read from Kipling, Dickens or some other well-known author.

Here we also got nature study and were taken for long walks around the area which suited me fine as I would willingly have done nothing else. There was even a small garden in which were grown vegetables and flowers. I little knew then, as my class helped with the weeding etc., that for well over thirty years I would be employed as a gardener in various parts of Scotland and the islands too.

I also recall some of us getting into trouble by daring each other to grasp hold of an electric fence a farmer had put up just outside the school. It was, indeed, only a mild shock, but we were soon taught that it was not something we should do again ... or the next shock would come as the headmaster's strap landed with some force on our bare hands.

Then one cold winter's day the measles came to call. Auntie Mary was staying with us at the time and the whole household went down with them except Dad. Rose took them first so that by the time I became ill she was well enough to be of some assistance to our harried father. Hamish was also beginning to be well again by then.

The measles seemed to haul off and clobber me and for several days I was very ill, delirious and semi-conscious. Only two things do I clearly recall from those days: one was that Hamish came into my sick room and gave me some toys he knew I liked; then there was the time someone, either Dad or Auntie Mary, came to say, "The King is dead."

This was, of course, said to my mother, who was in the room with me, but it was during one of my more lucid moments and I understood.

What I didn't know until later was that the doctor had decided to hospitalise me. One day he came to tell Dad that he had arranged for an ambulance to come from Lerwick, about twenty-five miles away, whilst he took me in his car to meet it. Put like that it sounds quite reasonable until you learn that we were in the middle of a fierce snowstorm with almost blizzard conditions all over Shetland.

The good doctor was somewhat surprised by the firmness of Dad's opposition. "What?" he cried. "If you do that the boy could easily catch cold just being carried out to your car ... and there's no saying that you and the ambulance will ever meet up ... John Arnold will stay right where he is ... in the warmth of his own home, with his own family around him."

As things turned out the doctor's car got stuck in the snow after travelling but a few miles, and the ambulance met up with whiteout conditions and came to a halt somewhere south of Lerwick.

I reckon I was very lucky that on seeing the dangers Dad had the strength of character to prevent the doctor's plan from being carried out.

In a way the measles did me quite a lot of good. Up until that time I had a lot of chest trouble, every time I got my feet wet I was wheezing, and as my feet were seldom out of water or wet ground I was always 'chesty', but after recovering from the measles I could get as wet as I wanted without ever suffering a wheeze.

We were all sorry about the death of the King but were too deep in our own troubles to dwell for long on the Royal Family and their sorrows. We were, like many others at that time, deeply interested in the monarchy and followed their lives in the newspapers. We children were probably all little royalists at that age and simply adored the new Queen and her children.

Dad was soon to give up farming work and find a job on the

island of Unst, only coming home at the weekend. This meant that he did not get home until late on Saturday night and was gone again on Monday. He may have been earning more money, but we missed him during the week and would rather have had him home all the time.

One Friday night Sheila, on being let out for a run before bedtime, did not return. Of course we were in bed, but after calling for her for some time Mum decided there was nothing to be done but teach the runaway a lesson by shutting her out and going to bed. In the night she thought she heard Sheila bark and got up to let her in, but there was no sign of her anywhere.

Next morning, when she still didn't appear, Mum became sure that she had crossed the Pool when the tide was out and now, for some reason, could not return. Although she did not voice her thoughts to us she became sure that something had happened to Sheila and she knew that some people were in the habit of setting rabbit traps in the sand dunes.

Hamish was back up in Yell again so there was only Rose and myself with her. That Saturday she kept us close to the house but we spent much of the day shouting Sheila's name in the vain hope that she would hear us and come home. We could not believe that our beloved Sheila could be dead somewhere, and came up with many unlikely explanations for her disappearance: she had gone back to live at the farm; she'd returned to her birthplace; she'd been kidnapped. But when I came up with the idea that pirates had come in the night and taken her away I was told not to be silly and stop frightening my little sister.

We could hardly wait for Dad to come home so that he could go and find her, but by the time he arrived it was dark and he could do nothing until the morning.

On the Sunday morning Dad set out to search for her and I was pleased when he allowed me to go with him. We went around the Pool rather than across it and I knew Dad was dreading what we would find. I know I was.

On the way we paused to speak to Uncle Jamie as we passed by his door.

"Ah, well," he said, "twice I've heard a dog barking over that way, both Friday night and last night."

"About the same place?" asked Dad, a scowl forming on his brow.

"Just about," Jamie said. "She might be in a trap."

Dad hated traps and snares and did not think very highly of those who set them.

Now he said coldly, "If Sheila's in a trap then the fellow that set it better look out."

We left Uncle Jamie and continued on our way. Dad's face had a thunderous look about it so I began to feel sorry for the fellow who had set a trap that caught our Sheila. At the same time I was thinking that if she had been heard barking just a few hours ago then she might still be alive.

"Dad," I said, "if Sheila's been caught in a trap will she be dead by now?"

The thunder left his brow as, smiling down, he replied, "I don't think so. Never you worry John Arnold, we'll find her ... and we'll find her in time. Only, she might be hurt bad so when we do find her let me handle her, for if she's in pain even Sheila might bite."

We did not cross the main runway but kept to the north side. Then suddenly Dad cried, "There she is!"

I looked to where he pointed and saw, a little way ahead of us, our poor dog limping along amongst the grass covered hummocks, having at last managed to free herself from the stake that had held her prisoner. She was not aware of us until we called her name. How horrified we were to see that clamped on one of her front paws was a ferocious looking gin-trap.

Dad swore bitterly, cursing the person who set those evil traps. Sheila was obviously exhausted and came towards us slowly, painfully, but showing her teeth in a welcoming grin. She also looked very guilty, as if she expected to get into trouble for running away.

Dad spoke gently to her as he bent down to remove the trap from her leg, which she let him do with only a shiver and a low growl at the pain of it. All this time we knew that the fellow who set the trap was watching us through binoculars from his window, so Dad took the trap and stake and, whirling them several times above his head, threw them far out into deep water. That trap would catch no more innocent creatures.

Without more ado he picked Sheila up and carried her all the way home again, stopping for a brief moment to exchange a few words with his brother as we passed by the cottages. As it turned out, Sheila's leg was not broken and in a few days she was her old self again. Though, mind you, whenever she wanted sympathy in future days she was inclined to limp.

Chapter Fourteen

The Lone Voyager

It was really fine to see Sheila running wide circles on the sand again. Boy! Could she run! I suppose it was a good way of giving her lots of exercise and she enjoyed every moment of it ... and so did we.

At that time our neighbours had a flock of hens that were ruled over by a very ferocious cockerel. This fine fellow did not confine his bullying to the hen run, but attacked any creature that came his way. He was Cock o' the Walk and meant that every other animal or bird on the island should know it. We children were warned to keep away from him as he could have done us serious damage.

Then one fine day he flew at our mother but she managed to get away from him without injury. When Dad was told about this attack he smiled grimly and said, "Just let him try that wi' me."

We all wondered what our fearless father would do. Would he kill the wicked, bossy bird? We were soon to find out.

A few days later Dad was walking along when he saw the cockerel prancing toward him. He knew the bird was intent on attack and determined to teach him a lesson. So, waiting until his feathered opponent leapt at him with beak, claws and leg spurs ready to tear flesh, he shot out a fist in a splendid uppercut.

Not for nothing was Dad acknowledged to be the best boxer in the family. Once, just before the war, he had sailed on a ship called the *Silveray* with an American ex-boxer called Joe Brieux and had learned his lessons well. Now the cockerel found that where humans were concerned he was certainly not top bird.

After picking himself up from where he landed he looked dazedly up at Dad before turning away and staggering back to the hen run. Never again did he try to bully human beings, but he remained quite a bossy bird amongst his feathered friends.

We often listened to programmes on the radio and enjoyed many of the favourite comedy and music shows of the time, but perhaps the one we liked best of all was the Scottish dance music on Saturday evenings. Sometimes, when the band struck up, the table would be pushed back for thirty minutes of energetic dancing.

Then there was also the news and weather forecast. It might be a little doubtful if the weather forecasted would come our way, but we always listened, and I suppose, as often as not, it did. The news was different, as we loved to hear what was going on in other parts of the world and would follow some stories eagerly ... such as the saga of the *Flying Enterprise*. We were thrilled by the bravery of the captain who would not leave his ship, and the courage of the tugboat skipper who joined him in an attempt to bring the ship to port, and were saddened when their attempt failed.

We had also followed news stories about the Korean War and, with many others, had worried that it might spread to become another World War.

We were well up with all the popular songs and sometimes when we went to town would return with the sheet music of the ones we liked ... anything from Scottish to cowboy and the modern tunes of the day. Perhaps the favourite during our years in Virkie was Ronnie Ronalde's 'If I were a blackbird', which we sang so often it is a wonder we were not told never to sing it again.

Once, we managed to persuade our mother to come to the hall to see the film 'Annie Get Your Gun', and this became one of our favourites. The hall was out Scatness way, to the west of the airport, and we often went there when concerts were on. Otherwise it was not an area we visited very often, but Uncle Jamie had a shed out that way in which he worked a loom and sometimes we'd go there with Dad and our uncle. Little did we know as we played about Scatness that under our feet lay the ruins of a Pictish settlement, which would one day become an important archaeological dig.

The 'Raft' made quite a difference to our roaming about the seashore and, even if I was not supposed to use her unless Hamish was there, I could at least sit on her deck when the tide was in and dangle my feet in the water. Sometimes I would, on finding her pulled up on the beach, pull her down again and sit on her after first making sure her mooring rope was securely tied to a stone. However, the problem came when I tried to return her to where I'd taken her from ... even though I was fairly strong it was quite a task and in the end I gave up pulling her anywhere. It was just as well that I didn't actually try to pole her around the Pool for, as the following story shows, there were dangers enough if you got into deep waters.

One fine day Hamish set out on his own to pole around the Pool. We had never actually tried to visit all the Pool on her, being content to stay about our usual haunts. Now Hamish decided to voyage further and as he poled determinedly towards the mouth of the Pool we, standing on the shore, watched worriedly as it appeared to us that he was going too far out.

Suddenly life on board the raft had more than a little danger to it when he found that his pole could no longer reach the bottom ... he was at the mercy of the wind and waves. Luckily neither was very strong at that moment but the danger was there as the raft was being drawn toward the more violent waters of the North Sea.

Hamish knew the danger. Had he been able to swim he could have gone into the water either to swim ashore or tow the raft into shallower waters. However, as a non-swimmer he had no choice but to stay with the raft come what may.

On shore we were now shouting at him to come back in, not realising that at this stage in his voyage he could not do so.

Out on the raft, Hamish was finding that the nearer he got to the entrance, the rougher the sea became, but he knew enough about the sea and boating to know that if he could not touch the bottom he must use the pole to scull the raft into safety. Slowly, using the pole in this way, he managed to work his craft along until he made landfall on the south shore, not far from where we found Sheila with the trap on her leg. From there he made his way into shallow waters and eventually returned to the tiny pier just below the house.

Hamish had not been in the least worried or frightened during this experience, but was exhilarated by the whole adventure. He had enjoyed himself immensely and was proud that he had succeeded in what he had set out to do, and had the seamanship to get himself out of trouble when it came. That might all have been true but he knew better than to tempt fate by setting out on such a trip again.

After that I recall no more stories about that fine vessel, so perhaps adult feet were put firmly down regarding our indiscriminate voyaging about the Pool. Of course, another explanation for this could be the fact that some time after this event Hamish left school and returned to Yell, where he was soon employed in the building of the new Mid Yell pier at Linkshouse.

Popeye, my rabbit, sometimes escaped and hopped around until caught and returned to his hutch. Being friendly with Sheila, and our felines Louise and June, he feared no dog or cat, which was to prove his undoing. One night he managed to escape and did not return. We learned later that he had met up with a dog belonging to one of our neighbours, and on running up to it was promptly killed. I grieved deeply at the terrible death of my friend.

I realised then that, while it had been fun to take Popeye into the house with the dog and cats, it had been a bad mistake as long as there was a chance he might escape and meet other carnivorous animals.

Dad was still working in Unst and the fact that he had to travel over three islands and the length of Shetland to get home to his family at the weekend was not something he was going to endure for much longer.

Then came the day when the news was broken to us that in a short time we were to leave Virkie and all our friends there, and move to Lerwick where we were to stay in Market Street.

Appalled by this dreadful news I took myself off to walk alone on the beach. Everything about the Pool seemed to stand out more clearly that day and it was all so very dear to me. I went along to where the 'Raft' lay up above the high water mark and sat down on its deck.

I did contemplate putting her into the water to have one last pole around the place, but realised in time that the tide was on its way out and I would look very silly sitting on a raft on several acres of dry sand.

Then high above the Pool I saw a rain-gös (red-throated diver) flying northward and wondered if everything was going to Lerwick. I looked down at the beach again and felt a little better when I saw a few plivvers (plovers) running about on the sand, and further away a group of gulls were sleeping as they stood with one leg tucked up into their feathers and their heads in their wings. There were other birds including shalders (oyster catchers) and ebb-pickers (turnstones) and it seemed as if I was noticing them for the first time although I knew they were there every day, taken for granted, and barely seen by us as we played on the sand that was their food store.

I think it was only at that moment that I really began to appreciate just what the Pool had meant to us, or at least to me. I was going to miss its soft sands when my feet were forced to walk the hard pavements of Lerwick. Then a horrible thought came to my mind ... would I have to wear shoes ALL the time in town?

In due course we journeyed up to Lerwick to view our new abode. As we walked along the grey streets I kept asking myself how anyone could enjoy living in such a place, where there were only stone walls with cramped little gardens in front of houses which all looked much the same ... I was ready to dislike the house in Market Street as soon as I saw it.

Strangely that did not happen. 17a turned out to be the tallest house in the street ... surely a mark in its favour. We were to live in the ground floor flat which was entered through a door at the back. I was pleased to see, once we went around the corner, that there was a good sized green with a row of sheds along one side, and best of all, a large free-standing elder tree at the bottom by the wall.

Whilst I disliked the idea of leaving Virkie to live in a town I did realise that there were several points in Lerwick's favour ... there were shops and the North Star Cinema to name but two.

I had always enjoyed films when they were shown in the local hall and would often lose all shyness in my eagerness to tell those who had stayed at home everything that had happened on the screen.

So now that we had been to Lerwick and seen the house we would be moving into very soon, and compared it to our little house in East Shore, it seemed huge and even I found myself sometimes wishing we could move in sooner. There was a great adventure ahead for us and, much as I hated leaving the Pool and our friends there, I longed for the new and interesting times to begin.

I did think it would be a good idea to put the raft back into the water before we left so that we could always think of her floating around forever in the Pool. Then I thought how we too were like rafts in a pool, always floating on from place to place, but never staying anywhere for long.

Chapter Fifteen

Life in Lerwick

As time went on I was to find that living in Lerwick was far more interesting that I had imagined, even if my first day at school was blighted, by having my ears boxed for not having gym shorts with me.

Yet I found the teachers in Lerwick Central to be, on the whole, far more caring and understanding than some I had met elsewhere, and they would take time to help you through difficult lessons. Of course to me, little school hater that I was, most lessons were difficult. During my years there, however, I really did begin to learn and ended up being first in art, second in history, third in geography and at, or near, the bottom of the class in those subjects I was less interested in.

Here the hatred I'd always felt for school began to lessen into dislike and there were times when I actually enjoyed myself. Like many other boys, however, I sometimes found myself in trouble for misbehaving in class, and at least once was, with several other lads, sent up to visit the headmaster, Mr Blance. As I can't recall his giving us the strap we must have been let off that time with a severe talking-to. I must admit though that I was once or twice given the strap and very likely earned every finger-numbing blow ... it did me no harm apart from a little pain and more probably did a lot of good.

I had made some good pals at the Central, which helped me to become less shy and slightly more outgoing, but the shyness would stay with me into manhood.

I was worried one day during my last term when one of our teachers, Mr Nicolson, came up to me and asked if I wouldn't like to stay on at school for an extra year or so. My reply was, "No, I don't think so," and I wondered if perhaps they would persuade my parents that I should, but I was allowed to leave when I was fifteen. Later, after I'd left, I did realise that he had been right and another

Louise 1950 – 1964.

year at school would certainly have done me no harm. I had no wish to return to a classroom although I realised that because of my inattentiveness my learning was not complete. So for the next few years I took only educational books out of the public library ... not that it helped much in some subjects which my mind just could not concentrate on, like maths, and I'm still not much good with figures.

I can't say that playing ball, or whatever, in Market Street was better than it had been on the sands of the Pool but we enjoyed ourselves well enough. We were often joined in our game by new friends, including George from a couple of doors down the road, and Eddie from further up. Sometimes though, the most enjoyable times were had in the house itself.

We had always been inventive in our play and perhaps that is how we came to turn part of our living room into a rather hilarious courtroom. Hamish was usually the judge, our friend John, now also living in town, would appear for the prosecution, whilst I would be the defence counsel. Often our roles would be reversed, but I always remember Hamish as judge. Sometimes other friends would be involved and great fun was had by all.

These 'trials' would involve any poor creature or person that took our fancy. Family members were often condemned to strange sentences and bizarre executions, which they seemed to survive very easily and with speed.

Louise or June were regularly charged with feline crimes. Having lost a tooth or two over the years Louise often sat by the fire with protruding tongue as if mocking us. She was swiftly charged with insulting behaviour and sentenced never to eat fish again. (Members of the court were not heard to object when the very next day she was fed a large portion of haddock.)

Another time, when she had a kitten, Louise was seen 'escorting' a man and his German shepherd dog away from her 'patch'. She followed them up the street until they turned the corner at Ganson's shop, whereupon she hissed after them, flexed her claws and swaggered back to where her pure white kitten, Nuikance, sat waiting on a wall.

John A.W. Strachan with June.

Louise was shortly afterwards charged with throwing her weight about and bullying a man and his dog. Upon being sentenced to life imprisonment in a dog kennel, the accused was seen to stick out her tongue at the judge who immediately charged her with contempt of court. An attempt to apprehend the accused failed when she suddenly jumped up and escaped via the newly opened door.

With June, whom I'd taught to come to me when I snapped my fingers, I could have even more fun when she was accused of some crime. As defence counsel I could make matters worse by changing my position and snapping my fingers. She would come and jump up onto my lap thereby causing the judge and prosecuting counsel some irritation.

The star of our animal trials was, of course, Sheila, who was

Walkies. Sheila takes us for a walk.

often accused of being prejudiced against poor, strange and, possibly, homeless cats that came anywhere near our back garden. Such vagrant animals would be chased relentlessly over nearby corrugated iron shed roofs making a great din and racket with her claws on the iron.

Sheila was always an ideal prisoner for she would sit there listening to the proceedings with her head tilted to one side or the other, depending on who was speaking, as if she was taking in every word, and, being of a nervous disposition was given to grinning in doggy fashion at whoever was addressing her.

The judge would glare at her, saying, "Sheila, you have been charged with a string of offences including that you, on numerous occasions, have left dirty, rotten, much-chewed bones lying where visiting people might trip over them, thereby causing hurt and possible contamination to our welcome guests ... how do you plead, guilty or not guilty?"

Sheila would immediately grin at him and the court would agree that the plea was 'not guilty' and the trial would begin.

The counsel for the prosecution would set out in detail all the charges against her, adding a few more he'd just thought up, and she would grin nervously at him, too.

Then the defence would rise and attempt to tear the charges to pieces. "Are there any witnesses who saw with their own eyes the bitch, Sheila, leaving the said bones about the place? Or who saw her chasing stray cats? Personally, I find it difficult to believe that such a fine dog as Sheila would ever commit such dastardly crimes."

If she was lucky no one would come forward as witnesses and the defence would quickly demolish the case against her, but in the end she would bare her teeth in a grin at the judge and be charged with contempt and given a 'never to be enforced' sentence.

Some trials would only last minutes, but others could be longer depending on the eloquence of those involved and the number of the charges.

I think we all enjoyed the trial of Old Willa, our neighbour. She was an octogenarian lady who had more sense of fun in her little finger than most people experience in a lifetime. However, she was so superstitious that had she lived a few centuries ago she would have been a sure candidate for the fires of Gallows Hill.

She never entered or left our abode without fondling the light switch, patting the door jambs and stepping only on certain squares of the lino. Nor did she ever leave without what we hoped were muttered blessings.

Often in the evening Willa would come to visit with her makkin, as would some other ladies, and on one such evening we decided to try her for witchcraft. As the old lady was sitting knitting with the other ladies chattering amongst themselves we did not ask her how she pled, but took it for granted that she would deny everything anyway.

Rising, the prosecution counsel cleared his throat and, avoiding our mother's frown, began: "I will attempt to prove to the court that the accused is indeed the most terrible of witches and is criminally superstitious. In fact, such is her superstition that when walking down the street she will not step upon the lines between the paving slabs, but plays a sort of hopscotch as she goes. I hope to prove that the accused often abandons the pavement altogether and puts vehicle drivers at risk by walking in the middle of the road.

"Your Honour, this woman is so immersed in magic and superstition that each time she enters the house she has certain places upon which she must place her hands or fingers. Also, she reads tea cups and uses other forms of divination on her unsuspecting victims."

Witnesses were called, possibly Rose and some other pals who stated that they had seen the said witch do all these things and more.

"Mi Lord," the defence counsel now addressed the judge, "this is but a dear old lady here, not some vile monster. So, what if she won't step on the lines on the pavement? Why, who knows what Godless mess lies between the cracks?

"So she walks on the street? Why not? We've all done it at some time or other. Yea, and when she does so the only one in danger is herself. Yes, Mi Lord, and if she touches things could it not be from exhaustion after all that hopscotch ... she might well be

Daa, our mother, Uncle John Leask, Dad and Louise.

clutching at walls and doors to keep her from falling down.

"I would like this court to realise that the only reason she reads tea-leaves in cups is that she is asked to do so by foolish and superstitious people. It is my firm belief that this fine old lady is innocent of any crime and if you are going to find her guilty this court is definitely misguided and prejudiced. Anyway, you're likely not going to listen to me ... so let's get on with it."

After that it took us only minutes to prove his last statement right and for the judge to sentence her to be taken out into the back green and burned. On hearing that the defence counsel's only comment was, "Right, wha's got the matches?"

I must add that Willa laughed as loud as anyone else, but I did notice that Mum was not amused ... it was no way to treat her guests.

Willa was always ready for a laugh. One day when Uncle Bertie dropped some tiny thing on the floor and was on his hands and knees searching for it, she suddenly leapt on to his back, slapped him on the rump and shouted, "Ride 'im cowboy. Yippy-yip!"

Everyone laughed, and beaming at us she declared that she would soon have him broken to the saddle and out for a gallop.

There were many such incidents during those years and she often had our house ringing with laughter on her evening visits.

Sometimes, instead of going to the shops herself she would ask one of us to go for her. She was once annoyed with me because, on being sent for a 'Kit Kat', I returned with a bar of chocolate instead of the tin of cat food she required for her cat's dinner. But my mistake did not stop her from dropping the 'e' from her favourite brand of cat food in the future.

Then, one mild New Year's day, she turned to me in the jollity of our living room and demanded a New Year kiss.

"Nae blink-

Willa with another welcome visitor to 17a,
Johnnie Mundie

142

in' fear," said I, as jumping up I headed for the door. Imagine my alarm when she followed, arms held out like some lovelorn Shakespearean actress.

Outside, I ran for the tree at the bottom of the green, but, kilting up her skirts she ran after me, eyes alight and twinkling with the thrill of the chase. I went up that old elder tree like a squirrel. Then, balancing on a branch, looked down to see this redoubtable old lady begin to climb after me.

I left the tree in a flying leap that took me onto the bordering wall and from there into the next street via someone's driveway.

As I went I could hear her laughter and cry of, "Come back an' kiss me."

Whilst I knew that she had chased me out of pure fun, I was on tenterhooks for a long time after that when she was near, for she gave me fair warning that she would claim her kiss when she got the chance.

Some months later, at a party, I became sleepy and dropped off whilst lounging on a settee. Presently I became aware of something pressing down on my face. I opened my eyes to behold the lined and unhandsome visage of the old wife bending over me.

"Ha, ha! Me boy," she cried, "I'm gotten dee noo! I telt dee I would!"

As the haze of sleep swiftly fled I realised that she had kept her word and claimed her kiss ... I was somewhat thankful that I had been asleep and had no memory of the experience.

When, some years later, the old lady departed our company she left a gap that could never be filled and, on looking back with memory's eye, I feel no little affection for the woman who, in old age, once chased me up a tree.

There were plenty of other characters about in those far off days including Charlie, an elderly gentleman who stayed with us for a few weeks. He had a large nose and an even larger thirst so that one morning, after a night on the tiles, he cut himself shaving.

"Run down to the chemist's and get me an antiseptic pencil," he said to me.

I agreed and hastened on my errand. However, during my

time in the shop I became a little mixed-up with rather drastic results. On my return I gave him the pencil and left him to it. It was only when I saw him again that I realised my mistake … instead of an antiseptic pencil I'd bought a caustic pencil.

Unaware of this error Charlie had treated his wounds and now he sported many black marks on his face. The trouble was, he hadn't only treated his shaving cuts but almost every other blemish on the skin, including several on his nose.

Although he didn't say much about it I think he thought me guilty of playing jokes on him, but I didn't … honest!

Another occasional visitor to 17a was old John, and though we might not see him very often we could be sure there would be a bottle or two of his homemade wine hidden in the deep pockets of his large raincoat. I think we all realised that the wine was only secondary and that company was really what he desired.

He was a tall, gentlemanly old fellow with a pointed snowy beard and an educated manner of speech. He would gladly accept a cup of tea and a biscuit and sit and chat for a while, but before he decided to take his leave out would come the bottle.

"I've brought along a bottle of my latest batch of elderflower wine," he might say, "just to see what you think of it."

There was no escape then. Every adult in the room had to sample the offering … not that there was anything wrong with it. In fact it was acknowledged to be a splendid drink, but was inclined to be very potent so that by the time he left, those who had joined him in a dram were feeling decidedly tipsy.

The house in Market Street was a haven for many people, especially those visiting Lerwick from Yell, and there was rarely a time when someone, either friends or family, was not staying overnight or longer. They were welcome and we enjoyed their company. There was always music and song and as the radio was still king we listened to many programmes. There was also a radiogram so we could play records or, on occasions when the lifeboat was called out to some vessel in distress, we could listen to all that went on on the 'trawler' wave band.

So, all in all, life was fairly interesting in town and we even enjoyed some of the hard winters we got back then. If we were in school when the snow started we'd watch the schoolroom windows eagerly after the first flakes were seen, hoping that if the fall was heavy we'd be sent home.

Even sledges were different in town. In Virkie our sledge was steered by having movable front runners, the boy steering sat forward with his feet on the front part and controlled the sledge with them. This worked quite well, but in Lerwick the only sledges I saw were built in one piece and were steered from behind, usually using the best clothes props as a rudder. We used to say that all we required were good runners and a fine long pole, but woe betide the boy who lost his ... mothers were not very understanding about lost clothes props, especially on their next washing day.

During our first winter Hamish made us a new sledge, large enough for three, or four if one stood at the back to steer, which was not easy to do. This sledge was fine on snow but uncontrollable on ice, as I discovered one evening some years later when I lost control on black ice going down Breiwick Road. I just managed to throw my female companion and myself off before the sledge disappeared over the banks. It was presently rescued from the beach undamaged, but I sledged no more on black ice.

It would not be possible to sledge now where we did in the 1950s as the volume of traffic is so much greater. Even then, though, there was an element of danger when using some of the streets and I remember well the crowds of lads and lassies on the corners shouting to warn sledgers that cars were approaching. Over the years they must have prevented a number of serious accidents.

Of course, some bairns did get hurt and there were many cuts and bruises, occasional broken bones and possibly splinters from crashing sledges. Whilst I did not suffer any serious injury I did, twice in the space of an hour, catch the fingers of my right hand between the sledge and the kerbstone, but we only stopped long enough for my pal's mother to treat the skinned knuckles.

Once a pal of mine was belly down on his sledge as it rocketed down Breiwick Road. Suddenly, to his horror, he found himself rushing towards a large army lorry. All he could do was hug his sledge and try to lie as flat as he could, as he disappeared underneath ... luckily he came out the other end unscathed and excitedly kept on sledging for the rest of the evening.

I recall one evening I went with Hamish and an Aberdonian friend of his, Freddy, to sledge in Gilbertson Road. We had both had a shot and just managed to get around the corner at the bottom. Then we gave Freddy a chance at steering. I was on the front, then Hamish, with the untried driver at the back with his pole.

Perhaps it would have been wiser to let Freddy practise on a less steep road, but by the time we realised that, we were hurtling down the road at a good rate of knots ... straight for the telegraph pole outside the Co-op shop. There was no hope of the sledge getting around the corner and, seconds before we hit the pole, I threw myself off expecting them to do likewise ... they didn't.

When I picked myself up it was to discover Hamish and Freddy wrapped around the telegraph pole. Slowly and painfully they disentangled themselves but we found that, apart from a few knocks and bruises, they were all right. They were lucky they'd hit the pole and not the stone wall behind it.

The sledge had not been so lucky for it had hit the pole with such force that two boards were broken off the front. Undaunted, we put the boards over a low wall and went up for another run. This time, when we arrived at the corner and attempted to turn, the pressure on the left runner was so great that it split from bow to stern and tipped us into the road. So, all we could do was drag the bits home to be repaired in time for our next bout of sledging.

Most roads and streets were uncomplicated, seldom straight, but easy enough runs. Occasionally, though, there were those with a sting in the tail, where you had to use all your steering skills to avoid a sudden and possibly painful stop. Bell's Road was one of those, even if it was quite a good little run ... until you came around the corner at the bottom to be faced with three concrete posts with just enough space between them to steer a well-aimed sledge. It could be very painful if you misjudged and wrapped yourself around one of them, which happened to me on more than one occasion ... we were convinced the council, in all their wisdom, had put the posts there as

146

John Fraser gives us a tune.

a trap for unwary sledgers.

Once I was going down Breiwick Road alone when suddenly, out of the night, came a much larger and faster sledge with four or five people on it. It caught the back of my sledge a glancing blow with enough force to knock me head-over-heels.

I wasn't to be let off that easily though for I became entangled with the other sledge and was dragged at some speed down the road

Freddie Morris, John Williamson & Billy Guthrie in Lerwick, c.1955.

along the fence. It could have meant serious injury for me, and I swear my head bounced off every fence post for the next twenty or thirty yards, but when the fence came to an end I was cast aside like a bundle of rags to roll over and over before coming to a stop. When I staggered to my feet again the world seemed to be turning at high speed and the street lights and stars were kaleidoscoping around me. It is a wonder I was not knocked down again in my dazed state by other sledgers that were a blur in the night as they raced by me at good speed.

As my head cleared I found my steering pole sticking through the fence and saw, a little further down the road, my sledge being knocked about by almost everyone that went down.

Sledging was wild adventure, much fun, and had an element of danger upon which we thrived in those days. Mind you, sledging did not stop when we left school and some sledgers never really lost interest.

Snowball fighting was also good fun and there were many

pitched battles in various places in town, but I must admit to preferring a good sledge run any day.

Shortly after we moved to Lerwick we decided that the stories in children's books and magazines were not all that good. We agreed that we could do better ourselves and set out to prove it. However, after a few days Rose lost interest (Hamish was in Yell at this time) and gave up trying, but something had clicked in my mind and from then on the only thing I wished to do was write.

Even though my writing then was what might be termed atrocious, and my spelling certainly not very good, I spent nearly all my spare time writing, at least when I was not at the North Star Cinema, lost in the actions of those heroes of the silver screen.

My aim was to write adventure stories and tales of cowboys in the American West, but I took so long to tell a story that very few were actually finished. It was to be quite a few years before I learned how to go over what I'd written and edit out anything unnecessary to the story.

In my early teens I could have been termed a struggling writer going nowhere. How I wished I had stuck in at school and learned what all those strange punctuation marks really meant.

I was also interested in art and sometimes would lay aside my pen to take up the brush or pencil, but while I liked drawing and painting my real joy was to invent characters and weave a story about them. True, many of the stories were badly written with simple plots that took no great brainpower to think up, but I loved every moment of it.

There were, of course, breaks when we would head up to Mid Yell for holidays. Where Daa's old boat would once again row us off to the fishing. When we could ramble again in the hills, go to work in the peats or just roam about the beach or burns, which made us feel that everything was just as it had always been and would always be. Nothing would change ... we little knew that even we were growing and changing and before long these holidays and Daa's old boat would be things in the past.

Sometimes, too, I would stop whatever I was doing to remember another time. A time when far away to the south we ran and played and shouted and sang. Where the gentle winds blew and the sand felt firm and moist under our toes, and out on the water the waves lapped cheerfully along the wooden hull of a raft in the Pool.

The Strachan Family Tree

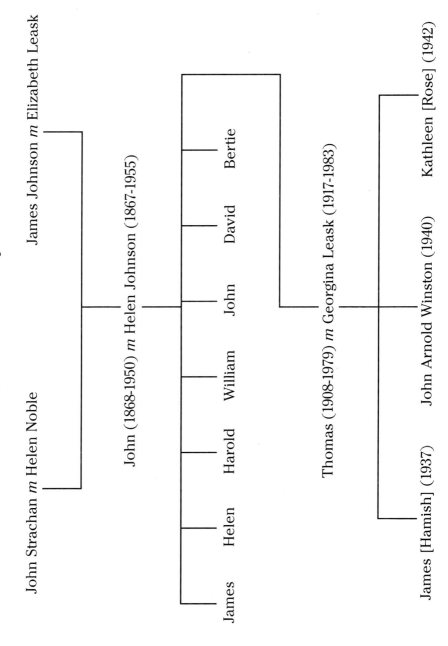

John Strachan *m* Helen Noble   James Johnson *m* Elizabeth Leask

John (1868-1950) *m* Helen Johnson (1867-1955)

James   Helen   Harold   William   John   David   Bertie

Thomas (1908-1979) *m* Georgina Leask (1917-1983)

James [Hamish] (1937)   John Arnold Winston (1940)   Kathleen [Rose] (1942)

The Leask Family Tree

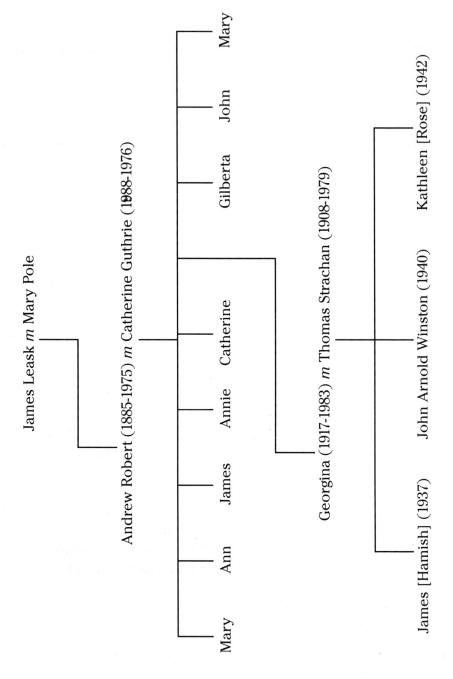

James Leask *m* Mary Pole

Andrew Robert (1885-1975) *m* Catherine Guthrie (1988-1976)

Mary   Ann   James   Annie   Catherine   Gilberta   John   Mary

Georgina (1917-1983) *m* Thomas Strachan (1908-1979)

James [Hamish] (1937)   John Arnold Winston (1940)   Kathleen [Rose] (1942)

Glossary

Aandoo	to row slowly against the current to keep a boat's position; row backwards gently
Bairns	children
Brunnie	a thick oatmeal scone
Crook	a hook above an open fire, from which pots were hung
Da	the
Daa	grandfather
Dat	that
Dem	them
Dirs (also ders)	theirs
Dunna	do not
Ebb-Picker	turnstone
Forkietail	earwig
Gansey	Guernsey, a knitted garment worn on the upper body
Hundiclock	great black beetle
Kishie	a basket made from straw
Krö (also spelt crö)	a sheepfold
Linns	short lengths of wood laid down on the beach to make pulling a boat up or down easier
Lioom	oily sheen on the surface of the water, often said to show where good fishing could be found
Makkin	knitting; (A makkin ... a group of knitters gathered in one building)
Mony	many
Mooritoogs	ants
Neesik (also neesick)	a porpoise
Noost	a place where boats are drawn up on the shore, above the high water line
Peerie	small

Piltock	a two- to four-year-old coalfish
Plivvers	plovers
Plucker	sea scorpion
Raep	a line for drying things on
Rain-gös	red-throated diver
Raise	to set wet peats on end to dry
Roog	to heap up peats
Shalder	oyster catcher
Sillock	coal fish younger than a piltock
Skadimans Head	sea urchin
Skrotti	a lichen
Slaters	woodlice
Steekit Stumba	a thick mist or fog
Sungaets	with the sun; clockwise
Sye	a scythe
Tink	think
Tilfers	the movable floor planking on the bottom of a boat
Trow	an elemental creature from folklore
Trysht	trouble or difficulty of some kind
Tushkar	an implement used for cutting peat
Widdergaets	opposite to the sun's movement; anticlockwise
Yis	yes